INNOVATION
Feast

Create new product ideas
to feed your hungry business

SUSIE WHITE

First published in 2018 by Grammar Factory Pty Ltd.

Printed in Australia by McPhersons Printing
Cover design by Designerbility
Book production and editorial services by Grammar Factory

A catalogue record for this book is available from the National Library of Australia

Disclaimer

For my wonderful girls, Holly and Sarah.
You're my best creations.

ABOUT THE AUTHOR

Susie White is a born-and-bred product innovator.

She started creating new products from a young age on her family's vineyard in rural Australia. Her first job was to crush grapes, stick down wine labels, and hot-seal foil lids on wine bottles. She witnessed firsthand the simple joy and pleasure people experience when they consume good food and drink. This set her on a lifelong journey into food and beverage product innovation.

For over fifteen years, Susie held leadership roles in innovation and marketing, developing new world-class product pipelines for multinational companies such as Colgate-Palmolive, Kraft Foods, Cadbury, Procter & Gamble and Mondelez International.

Susie is now a product innovation author, speaker and founder of Eat. Drink.Innovate, which helps businesses develop new product ideas to fuel their long-term growth. To date, Susie has generated more than 3,000 new product ideas and built new product pipelines worth over $800 million in sales for the businesses she works with.

Innovation Feast is Susie's first book. Presenting the very best of her innovation know-how, firsthand industry experience, and actionable learnings, she teaches food and beverage businesses how to grow using successful product innovation.

WHAT PEOPLE SAY ABOUT
WORKING WITH SUSIE

'Susie is great at pushing boundaries, getting the best out of people and thinking out of the box.'
Dan Tripolitano, Head of Insights and Innovation,
Treasury Wine Estates, USA.

'Susie's ideation workshops always encourage amazing creativity and strategic thought to keep teams upbeat and energised. Many of the outputs from these days are now real products on retail shelves throughout Australia and overseas. That is the ultimate endorsement!'
Rod Heath, Capability Manager, Food Innovation Centre,
Monash University.

'Susie is so easy to work with, there's no egotistical crap or BS, she listens and has a great feel for what is required to achieve the desired results. If you haven't gone through this process – do! It could save you a lot of money instead of developing products that no-one wants and that won't sell.'
Shila Barak, Business Development Manager, Well and Good.

'Susie is one of the best storytellers and strategic thinkers in the food innovation business. When it comes to developing and managing new products, she really knows what works.'
Ben Wicks, Global Brand Director, Mondelez International

'Susie has great activities and enthusiasm to help get your team into a new way of thinking about potential ideas and product solutions. I hadn't realised there was a whole structure to ideation – it was an inspiration.'

Dr. Hazel MacTavish-West,

The VegDoctor at MacTavish West Pty Ltd

'I needed to develop new products that fit the market.
Susie did everything she said she would, on time, on budget and at a really high standard. If you want someone professional who will get the job done, painlessly, work with Susie.'

Nicole Lamond, Director, Universal Village.

'Susie really knows her stuff and has a great sense of humour.
Her experience and expertise relating to food and beverage innovation is outstanding and comes from her heart. Key to this is how she works with teams, looks at the desired outcome, and delivers.'

Jane Cockburn, CEO, Kairos Now Pty Ltd

'Susie provided an innovation framework and developed a global innovation pipeline of products with us. She also trained super users to ensure the innovation capability was truly embedded in our organisation. The expert collaboration, support and creativity provided by Susie, exceeded all my expectations.'

Kirstie McCosh, Global Head of Marketing Services,

Treasury Wine Estates.

ACKNOWLEDGEMENTS

Thank you to all the businesses I've worked with who have gone on the exhilarating rollercoaster ride of creating new products with me. This book is for people like you, to help bring more delicious, desirable and inspiring food to our tables.

A big shout out to my business mentors at Dent Global who set my feet firmly on this path, especially Glen Carlson, Dave Dugan and Andrew Griffiths. Thanks to my business accountability group for their constant encouragement: Claire, Kate, Jordan and Lalita, it's been a pleasure to share this journey with you talented folks.

This book wouldn't be as smooth or as polished without the wisdom and guidance of the Grammar Factory team. Thank you to my editors, Jacqui and Michelle, for navigating the rough writing waters with me. And to Julia at Designerbility for the delicious looking book cover.

Thank you to my parents, Rod and Julia, for an amazing start to life on our family vineyard, and for being the first daring entrepreneurs I knew. My sister Ali, for offering help and rescue whenever I need it. And lastly, a heartfelt thank you to my husband Richard for his unflagging support; he is the rock to my roll, the constant to my change, and believes I can (and will) achieve everything I set my mind to.

CONTENTS

INTRODUCTION:

Fighting an Innovation Famine

Wanting something is not enough. You must hunger for it.
Your motivation must be absolutely compelling in order to overcome the
obstacles that will invariably come your way.'

– Les Brown

There is a burning need among food and beverage businesses to use product innovation to drive long-term growth. Yet, many businesses, like yours, may be struggling to do so, for a number of different reasons.

Perhaps what you've been doing simply isn't working anymore, and growth is stalling or going backwards. This is what I call an innovation famine, as your business is starved of growth.

These 'hunger pains' often lead to impatience from stakeholders, who have huge expectations about what you should deliver. This can lead to a panic, whereby new products are thrown into the market with wild abandon, in the hope that something will stick.

Or perhaps your business is experiencing an innovation glut. You've been growing steadily and have so many new product options that you don't know what to do next. Worried about making the wrong decision, you end up doing nothing. Or you waste a lot of time and effort trying to agree on which products to launch first.

Whether your business is experiencing an innovation glut or an outright famine, there is enormous pressure to come up with new and original product ideas. Product innovation is essential in helping companies achieve sustainable growth and profitability. A recent KPMG survey of senior executives within food and beverage businesses identified product innovation as their number one growth driver over the next one to three years.

Innovation also keeps food and beverage products relevant to shoppers, and satisfies their strong appetite for more choice. According to a Nielsen Global New Product Innovation Survey, sixty-three per cent of global consumers said they like it when companies offer new products, and sixty-nine per cent of Asia-Pacific consumers said they purchased a new product during their last grocery shop.

Yet, according to a study by the Product Development and Management Association (PDMA), about forty-five per cent of all new consumer products fail at launch. That statistic is pretty scary – especially when you're the one who is responsible for creating and launching new products.

Added to that is the sheer demand for food, which is only going to increase. According to CSIRO Australia, by 2050, the world's population is expected to increase from 7.1 billion to 9.6 billion, requiring a seventy per cent increase in the production of food. Globally, we will eat as much in the next four decades as we have over the past two hundred years.

However, people aren't willing to throw just anything down their throats anymore. Our blind faith in big food and beverage companies, with sophisticated manufacturing and processing, has been eroded. With the technology revolution – of global Internet access, smartphones and software apps – comes an accompanying thirst for greater knowledge, transparency and accountability in the quality, source and nature of the food and beverages we consume.

If you're a processed or packaged food producer, you may have copped a beating in recent times. Food manufacturers are coming under constant scrutiny to increase the transparency of ingredients, and reduce the use of additives and amount of processing. According to Euromonitor, the global packaged food industry grew by only one point one per cent in 2016, which represents a ten-year low. This compares to the fresh food industry, which grew globally by three per cent.

Food producers need to be smarter with their new product innovation efforts, because consumers now want it all. The traditional trade-off of convenient, fast food at the expense of fresh, nutritious food is over. According to Nielsen, the top four global future food needs are for products that are:

- Affordable.
- Healthy.
- Convenient.
- Environmentally friendly.

These needs are driving massive changes in food consumption, with people seeking fresher, more natural and less processed foods.

However, if you're a chocolate maker, don't despair and start dipping lettuce leaves in chocolate. The see-saw between consumers' desire for indulgent food versus healthy food remains in motion. According to Nielsen, global sales of healthy categories – like fruit, tea, vegetables and bottled water – grew by five per cent in 2016. This outpaced the two per cent growth of indulgent categories, like soft drinks, chips, chocolate and biscuits. However, both categories outperformed the semi-healthy categories such as juice, cheese, cereal, muesli and granola bars, which declined by one per cent. What does this mean? That there is room for both healthy and indulgent food in today's world. You just need to be very clear about which category you fall into, and the choices you're offering people.

That doesn't mean you can rest on your laurels, though. While processed food has several major benefits (including less food spoilage and contamination), all those additives used to lengthen shelf life, and artificially enhance the look and taste of food, now need to be replaced with healthier, more natural options. The ongoing industry innovation challenge is to find better alternatives. We need to deliver foods that are flavourful, nutritious, safe, convenient and affordable, while satisfying consumer expectations of year-round availability. The need to innovate, and create better food and beverages, has never been greater.

A Tailor-made Approach to Product Innovation

This book is designed specifically for food and beverage businesses – not for digital, software, financial or service-based businesses. These industries seem to have had a chokehold on innovation for the last decade, with a focus on methodologies like design thinking and lean start-up. While some of these approaches are useful for food innovation, many of them are not.

In software innovation, for example, there's a mantra that new products have to be '10X'. That means they must be ten times better than the ones they're replacing, in order to motivate people to make a permanent switch to buy them. For food and beverage products, successful innovation does not need to be so functionally radical or extreme. People's tastebuds don't change every six months, like computer software does. And while the majority of people would like technology to enable fresher, faster and healthier meals, the end product cannot be unrecognisable, Frankenstein-style food. Early consumer research into the acceptance of 3D-printed food found that most people preferred printing of already processed foods like chocolate or pizza, rather than the printing of natural or fresh products like meat from laboratory-cultured ingredients.

When it comes to food and beverages, people are looking for small but meaningful changes that will improve their health, make it easier to eat and prepare food, or simply add a little variety. The major purchase drivers of new food and beverages of affordability, convenience, brand preference and novelty have remained consistent for decades. However, a new set of purchase drivers – which used to be considered niche – are now increasingly becoming mainstream, such as, health and wellness, safety, social impact, experience and transparency. Fifty-one per cent of consumers in a 2017 Deloitte study said these new drivers play a significant role in their choice of food and beverages.

The goal of this book is to help you create the best scenario possible for your business – what I refer to as an innovation feast. If you follow the steps outlined in this book, you'll be able to create a menu of delicious new product options that you can browse and select from as your business grows. The tools and techniques I share are specially designed for creating innovative food and beverage products that people want to buy. It's my ambition that your new product innovation exceeds consumers' desires with the best food possible, rather than the latest fad or hack from Silicon Valley. Imagine a future in which there is no shortage of new products that your consumers really want, enabling your business to fuel its future growth ambitions.

But before I unveil the steps that will transform your business from an innovation famine to feast, allow me to explain who I am and how I can help you.

From Farm Life to Front-end Innovation

I got into product creation at an early age, while growing up and working on my family vineyard in Australia. We grew Chardonnay, Riesling, Cabernet Sauvignon, Merlot and Cabernet Franc wine grapes, and harvested them to sell to larger wine producers. For ten years as grape growers, my family was at the mercy of the weather, and the forces of market supply and demand. Not enough rain meant poor crops and low return. Too much rain meant mildew, bad crops and low return. Good weather caused an oversupply in grapes and low return. To escape this boom and bust cycle, my parents invested in wine-making equipment, became wine makers and built a cellar door on our vineyard.

This heralded the start of an annual, hand-operated wine production run. Mum would pour the hand-crushed wine into bottles and Dad would press in the corks. Then my older sister and I would stick on the labels and hot-foil seal the caps. My boyfriend (now husband) would then pack the bottles into boxes and load them onto pallets to store in the cellar.

Creating and selling our own family wine ignited my early delight with making delicious products that people really enjoyed. I just loved seeing the simple pleasure and joy people experienced when they consumed good food and drinks. This set me on a lifelong journey into food and beverage product creation.

I've been working in the industry trenches as an innovation manager for over twenty years now. I've worked in marketing and innovation roles within large, multinational consumer goods companies, such as Procter & Gamble, Colgate-Palmolive, Kraft Foods, Cadbury and Mondelez International, across Australia and Europe. In these roles, I increased new product idea success rates from thirty per cent to seventy per cent. To date, I've developed more than 3,000 new product ideas and generated new product pipelines worth over $800 million in sales.

Drawing on my industry knowledge and experience, I founded an innovation business called Eat.Drink.Innovate. I now help food and beverage businesses create their own new products for long-term growth. My speciality is the fast-moving consumer goods (FMCG) category, which is anything you buy from your local grocery or convenience store and consume or use regularly, such as bread, milk, biscuits, pet food and dishwashing detergent. Everything in this book is a skill, tool or technique I personally use and have achieved successful outcomes with. The information is based on my firsthand experience of what works and what doesn't in the real world of business, rather than what looks good in an agency credentials presentation.

Where a lot of businesses go wrong is skipping the first phase of innovation. Product innovation goes through two distinct phases of development – discovery and delivery. The discovery phase is known as the front-end of innovation. It's when you're starting out on your innovation journey. You know you need to create something, and you must work through a lot of uncertainty and ambiguity to identify what you should make. This chaotic stage is best represented by the squiggle shown in the following diagram.

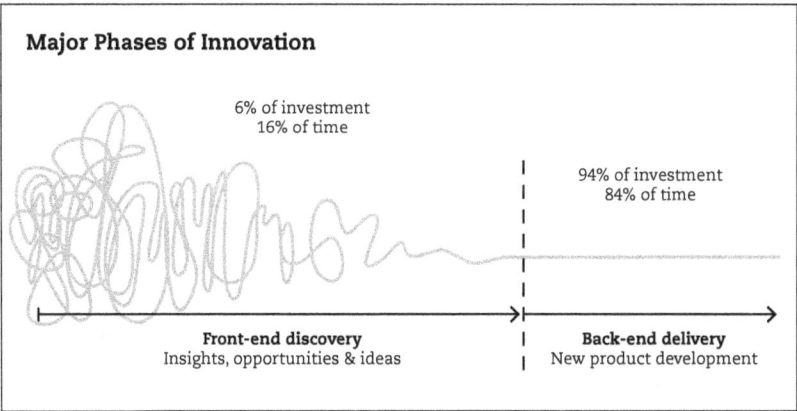

Major Phases of Innovation

6% of investment
16% of time

94% of investment
84% of time

Front-end discovery
Insights, opportunities & ideas

Back-end delivery
New product development

Source: *The Design Squiggle, Damien Newman, 2006*

Most businesses don't know about or understand the front-end discovery phase of innovation. They spend over eighty per cent of their time and ninety per cent of their money in the back-end delivery phase of innovation, by moving straight into developing and launching new products.

According to product innovation experts Robert Cooper and Elko Kleinschmidt, there are eight critical factors that will increase the likelihood of new product success.

1. Solid upfront homework: Scope and justify the project before you begin.
2. Voice of the customer: Gather customer inputs throughout the project.
3. Product advantage: Offer unique benefits and superior value for customers.
4. Early product definition: Be clear on your product offer before development begins.
5. Cross-functional team: Gain cross-functional support with a strong leader.
6. Well-executed launch: Secure adequate resources and execute effectively.
7. International orientation: Validate with multi-market research.
8. Right organisational structure: Secure top management support.

The first five of these critical factors for innovation success should be completed in the front-end of innovation *before* any product development starts. I've worked with many businesses that start their innovation in the back-end of innovation, leaping straight to making products in the hope that people will buy them. When in-market sales are poor, there's a trail of bewildered employees saying, 'But it tasted so good... I don't understand why it didn't sell.'

Does this sound familiar? If so, chances are you've been skipping the crucial front-end stage of innovation. That's like diving into a pool without bothering to learn how to swim first. The biggest and best secret to successful innovation is to find out whether you have a product idea that people really want *before* you invest a lot of time and money into making it. This is known as product-market fit. You're checking whether there is any appetite in the market for what you're offering. Are people really hungry for your new products? Or are you trying to cram something unwanted down their throats?

By taking the time to work through the front-end of innovation to understand your customers' needs, and clearly define a unique and superior product that suits these, you can significantly increase the likelihood of your in-market success.

By not checking product-market fit first, you're using a trial and error approach to product innovation. This is the most expensive and wasteful way to learn whether your new product will sell or not. At best, you waste a lot of time and money making a product that flops in-market. At worst, you damage your business long term by starving it of growth, while your customers start to wonder whether you know what you're doing. To determine market appetite, it's better to first identify a consumer opportunity, and create product ideas that you know will satisfy it, before you start making any new products.

That's not to say effective manufacturing, production, shipment, and launch support of new products isn't vital for new product success. On the contrary, there's no point having a good idea if the execution isn't outstanding as well. If you have the best product idea and don't execute it well, then that brilliance never sees the light of day. And vice versa – even with the most amazing launch execution, a poor idea is still rubbish and is quickly identified as such by today's discerning consumers.

There are many excellent books and resources that will teach you how to market, distribute, sell and promote your products. This book isn't one of them. This book focuses on finding and creating amazing new product ideas first. It's that chaotic, ignored and much-avoided front-end bit of innovation I want you to focus on. Once you get the product idea right, a brilliant launch execution can then follow.

Introducing the FEAST Framework

According to a survey by McKinsey, sixty-five per cent of business executives are only 'somewhat', 'a little', or 'not at all' confident about the decisions they make about innovation. Seventy-three per cent of the senior executives surveyed indicated that innovation isn't part of their formal strategic-planning process, while a third said they manage innovation on an ad-hoc basis when necessary. How can you expect innovation to be a key growth driver if it isn't an integrated part of your business?

An ad-hoc, unstructured approach to product innovation usually results in small, and incremental product improvements. To stretch beyond these, innovation needs to become recognised as a strategic growth driver in your business, with an intentional and repeatable process that creates products that consumers value. Some businesses fear that a fixed innovation process will shackle and constrain innovation. However, this leaves them reliant on gut instinct, blind luck and sheer willpower to see them through.

Ironically, when dealing with something as ambiguous, confusing and uncertain as the front-end discovery phase, a staged innovation process works like an absolute dream. It helps you stay disciplined and be guided by consumers to prove an idea's worth, rather than falling prey to the true enemies of innovation – assumption, opinions and internal lobbying.

This book is going to introduce you to a repeatable and sustainable five-stage innovation framework called FEAST, which stands for focus, explore, accelerate, sense-check and transform. It will create an innovation feast for your business by developing enough winning new product ideas to fuel your business growth for the next three years. By undertaking these five steps in other businesses, I've improved new product success rates by as much as fifty per cent.

This staged approach will help you answer some of your most burning questions, like:

- How much product innovation should I do?
- Where should I focus my product innovation efforts?
- How do I find new product opportunities?
- How do I choose the right new product ideas to develop?
- How can I track my innovation progress and success?

The five-stage FEAST framework will give your business the confidence and the know-how to develop the best product innovation ideas possible *before* you invest significant time and money in making and launching any new products.

This book is split into five sections, with each one covering a different part of the five-stage FEAST innovation framework outlined here.

THE FIVE-STAGE FEAST FRAMEWORK

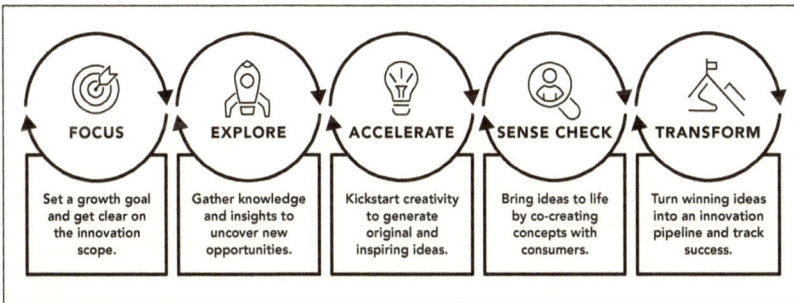

FOCUS	EXPLORE	ACCELERATE	SENSE CHECK	TRANSFORM
Set a growth goal and get clear on the innovation scope.	Gather knowledge and insights to uncover new opportunities.	Kickstart creativity to generate original and inspiring ideas.	Bring ideas to life by co-creating concepts with consumers.	Turn winning ideas into an innovation pipeline and track success.

There's also a Warm-up Stage, where you'll discover the most common innovation problems facing food and beverage businesses, plus how to build an innovation team to tackle the FEAST framework head on.

Remember, you are working in one of the most vital and growing industries in the world. Food and beverages have a huge impact on people's wellbeing and global sustainability. It truly is the stuff of life and death. Food provides the energy and fuel to sustain us physically and mentally. It also provides a social experience, helping us to celebrate and commiserate. As a food or beverage producer, you have the opportunity to be a pioneer in this space, offering more than just business profitability. You have the ability to change the quality of people's lives.

Let's get started.

WARM-UP STAGE:

Innovate or Fry

> 'They always say time changes things,
> but you actually have to change them yourself.'
> – *Andy Warhol*

These days, when someone says, 'You need to be more innovative,' it's hard to know what they mean or how you should do it. Because 'innovation' is used to describe many things – a behaviour, a mindset, a process, a technology, a culture… the list is endless. If you ask Google for an innovation definition, it comes up with over 300 million results.

I like the simple definition of innovation as 'change that adds value' because it has the two essential parts I've personally found to be vital. 'Change' means something happens to shift the status quo, while 'adds value' means the change that occurs leads to a better outcome. In the context of food and beverage products, this value might be financial value (which people will pay more for), functional value (which offers people tangible benefits like improved health, taste or ease of use) or emotional value (which makes people really want or like it).

This book is about new product innovation. Some businesses get a bit hung up on the 'new' part of product innovation. For our purposes, we'll define new product innovation as any product that a consumer hasn't purchased before. As you'll soon discover, there are many different types of new product innovation. This can range from changing ingredients and introducing new packaging to creating a totally new form of food or beverage.

The primary goal of new product innovation is to create, update or adapt a product so that it adds value to the people who use or consume it. This is important because a lot of businesses make new products, and change existing products, for the sake of change – *without* adding any real benefits or value for their customers. This is the biggest secret to innovation success and the core focus of this book: Make what people want, not just what you can make.

The purpose of this Warm-up Stage is to prepare you for the FEAST framework. I want to ensure you're in the best position possible to executive the five stages. In order to do that, there is some background information you need to be aware of, and some preliminary work you need to do. In the following section, you'll discover four common innovation problems food and beverage businesses face, and how to assemble an innovation team to tackle these problems and maximise your chances of new product success.

Four Common Innovation Problems

There's a great saying from Bill Gates: 'Success is a lousy teacher. It seduces smart people into thinking they can't lose.' What he meant is that once you do something well, you do it again and again, and assume that you'll keep being successful.

This applies to creating new products if you've already had some in-market success. Many businesses keep making what they know, until it all goes horribly wrong and they're forced to look for a new approach. Fortunately, these problems are predictable. Here are four of the most common problems I come across in new product innovation for food and beverage producers. By following the five stages of the FEAST innovation framework, you'll be able to avoid or overcome all four of them.

1. FLAVOUR FATIGUE

After launching and successfully selling a food or beverage product, many businesses choose the most obvious form of innovation – they make lots of different flavours or varieties of their original product. While their business grows at first, over time fewer people buy the new flavours, and retailers run out of extra shelf space. Growth slows, and the business is left with a huge range of product flavours or line extensions. Simply making new flavours doesn't seem to be the answer anymore, but the business doesn't know what else to make. This is like tipping sugar continuously into a cup of coffee. At first, you really notice the steady increase in sweetness, but it gets to a point where it's so sickeningly sweet that putting even more sugar into the cup has little to no discernible effect. The secret here is to understand that not all types of innovation are equal. You need to know what types of innovation there are, and how much of each you should be doing to grow your business.

2. CHURN AND BURN

Businesses that suffer from churn and burn are savvy and know they need to innovate. They spend a lot of time and money throwing new product after new product into the marketplace. Despite this, people aren't buying their new products, so they try more new offerings, still with limited success. Now they're worried, retailers are getting impatient, and the business is running out of ideas and money. It's like jumping in a high-performance, fuelled-up car and driving furiously at top speed, with no idea where you're heading. You end up tired, out of fuel and lost. The secret here is to co-create and optimise ideas with your consumers *before* you make anything, so you know you're heading down the right track.

3. EMPTY PANTRY

Many food and beverage businesses are crazy busy. Every dollar and employee is tied up in the day-to-day operations of the business, which just focuses on getting through the current month, let alone the full business year. However, panic hits when a retailer or stakeholder asks what the future growth plans are. The business suddenly realises it isn't sure how it will innovate beyond the next twelve months because there are no real plans in place. There's been limited long-term planning and resources dedicated to creating future growth options. This is like when your friends pop in for a visit and you open up the pantry to rustle up something to eat, only to realise you've got nothing to offer them. The pantry is bare and it's too late to run down to the shops to grab something. The secret here is building an innovation funnel that spans three years, which helps you align and prioritise your resources to deliver future business growth.

4. LEAKY BUCKET

These businesses love the lure of new things and pride themselves on their product innovation. They're happiest when creating the next big thing. In fact, they're so busy creating and launching new products that they start to neglect their existing products. Over time, these products become less relevant and outdated, so sales start to decline. Unfortunately, this part of the business is also their most profitable, so no matter how many shiny, new products they tip into the top of their sales bucket, they can't make up for the lost sales that are dripping out of the business faster. The secret here is to develop an innovation strategy that focuses on the right mix of new product *innovation* and core product *renovation*, so your growth and profit dependence is balanced across the business.

Now that you understand the four most common innovation problems food and beverage businesses face, you're almost ready to start tackling the FEAST framework. There's just one more thing you need to do first.

Assemble an Innovation Team

If you want to develop successful new product ideas to launch, there are two essential ingredients you need in addition to the FEAST framework. Those ingredients are people and time.

I was once invited to meet with a market-leading business about a global innovation project that they thought was off-track. When I was ushered into their boardroom, I braced myself to meet a massive innovation team. Instead, one concerned lady was sitting there. She was responsible for delivering the whole project, alone. I was amazed she wasn't lying comatose under the table. I resisted the temptation to give her a reassuring hug, and instead made sure that the first thing I did was recruit a team to share the load.

You cannot do product innovation alone.

Forget all those stories of fearless solopreneurs doing it alone. When you dig deeper, you realise that while they may have come up with an idea by themselves, many other people, who don't share the limelight, helped them turn it into a reality. If you truly want to succeed at product innovation, you need to become an 'intrapreneur'. That is, someone who drives innovation within, and for the benefit of, their business. To maximise your success, you need to assemble an innovation team.

WHO SHOULD I RECRUIT TO HELP ME?

Whenever I say, 'I'm creating new product ideas – would you like to join in?' I'm usually swamped with people wanting to help because it's fun, inspiring and empowering to create something new for the business you work in.

As the innovation project leader, you're looking to create a core innovation team who will experience every stage of the FEAST front-end journey with you. I suggest you gather a minimum of four people and a maximum of ten for your team. Any fewer and you'll struggle to get the breadth of input needed. Any more than ten people and it's like running a circus, with constant arguments over who is the ringmaster.

When recruiting people, first look inside your business. Ideally, you'd like a mix of cross-functional expertise from people who work *with* your consumers, or make things *for* your consumers. For example, someone from sales, marketing, consumer research, product development, and supply chain. This will ensure you have the diversity of expertise, and can tap into knowledge across the areas of your business that your new product ideas will impact the most.

Your innovation team members don't have to be the most experienced employees you have. Remember, these are your team members, not subject matter experts. In fact, it's better if they're the action-orientated 'doers' of your business, not senior-level thinkers. You want these people to share your innovation journey with you, by completing the actions in each FEAST stage, rather than delegating these jobs to others. If you're short of team members, try looking outside your business. Have you got any great suppliers you regularly work with or find particularly helpful and inspiring? These may be in packaging, ingredient supply, artwork design or advertising. As long as they're not in direct competition with you, they may be very interested in collaborating to support your business, as it may ultimately grow theirs. Having an external view is also invaluable for bringing in greater diversity of thought and broader industry knowledge.

And now the watch-out. If you and your working team are quite similar in terms of your values, experiences and perceptions, that creates a problem when you're trying to be innovative, because innovation thrives on diversity. It needs different people, thinking different things, to come together and make fresh, unexpected connections. The more unique and diverse your innovation team, the more diverse and unique your new product ideas will be. So, not only do you want differences in functional expertise, you also want to recruit a good mix of different ages, nationalities, gender and experience levels to maximise your innovation team's capabilities and diversity.

WHAT MINDSET SHOULD I LOOK FOR?

Apart from being different from you, your team needs to be open-minded. Look for the natural change agents. In every business, there are people wanting to change the status quo, who are bursting with ideas that no one usually listens to. I call these people yaysayers. Yaysayers are passionate about change and have a 'can-do' attitude. I'm not talking about blind optimism here; they see opportunities where others see barriers. To identify a yaysayer, simply ask: 'Do you have any ideas about how we could improve things in our business?' Yaysayers will drown you with ideas for improvements that they're bursting to implement. They naturally want to see things improve and are willing to overcome difficulty to see it through.

An example of this is Max Schubert, Penfolds' first chief winemaker. He combined traditional Australian wine-making techniques with inspiration from Europe to make the first experimental vintage of Penfolds Grange wine in 1951. After sharing his creation with the Penfolds board, he was ordered to shut down his experiment. For three years he continued to craft Grange in secret, hiding these vintages in the depths of the Penfolds cellar. Nine years after his first Grange production, the Penfolds board asked Schubert to restart production of Grange. Today, Penfolds Grange is one of Australia's most prized wines, with first vintages selling for more than $50,000 a bottle, that's about $10,000 a glass!

At all costs, avoid recruiting naysayers. Naysayers are those dogged realists who refuse to deal with anything beyond the immediate here and now. They're often so worn down and burnt out that cynicism clouds their every view. To identify a naysayer, ask the same question: 'Do you have any ideas about how we could improve things in our business?' You'll be overwhelmed with a bitter tirade of how bad things are, and a whinge-fest of all the problems they have to contend with daily – with no solutions on how things could actually be improved. Naysayers are so busy being devil's advocate, and pointing out all the flaws, that they struggle to focus on solutions. In early product innovation, naysayers will hold you back and keep you grounded in the current reality. They will be fearful of the unknown, and limit fresh thinking around what's possible by turning it back to: 'Here's what we can do right now.' This means you'll just keep coming up with the same stuff, made the same way you do right now. And that's *not* the definition of innovation.

HOW MUCH TIME WILL I NEED?

Unless you're working in a large business with dedicated product innovation managers, chances are that finding new product opportunities from scratch isn't your full-time role. Most small and medium businesses kick off an innovation project by asking an employee in product development, marketing or sales to go find 'the next big thing', on top of completing their day job. The team members you recruit internally or externally may also have other full-time work responsibilities. The key thing now is to determine how much time you can carve out to complete this innovation project.

You can run your innovation project as a sprint or a marathon. The five-stage FEAST framework can be done in as little or as much time as you have. It really depends how much effort you're willing and able to throw behind it. To give you a guideline, I've done it in as little as ten days when it was a burning priority and my team worked on worked on nothing else, and for as long as nine months when I was juggling four other live projects at the same time.

I suggest you maintain a healthy jogging pace and allow three months for completion. This will allow you enough time to work on your innovation project one to two days a week, and manage other work commitments for the other three to four days. It will allow your team to meet weekly, complete key action steps, and run the full-day workshops required at key stages.

You will need to be clear with your business managers about the time and effort you and your team require to complete your innovation project (in Stage 1, I'll advise you when to have this conversation). While your team might be personally excited and passionate about creating new product ideas, this isn't optional fun to be done outside of work. It's a business-critical project that will fuel your business's growth for the next three years. If that's not worth some dedicated time and effort, nothing is.

Key Learnings and Actions

Once you have an innovation team in place, and you've allocated a time-frame to complete the five-stage FEAST framework, you're ready to proceed to Stage 1. This stage is critical for getting you started on the right track, and focusing your innovation efforts in the best direction. But first, here's a summary of the key learnings and actions from the Warm-up Stage:

KEY LEARNINGS

- The primary goal of new product innovation is to create, update or adapt a product so that it adds value to the people who use or consume it. In other words, make what people want, not just what you can make.

- The four most common problems I come across in new product innovation for food and beverage producers are flavour fatigue, churn and burn, empty pantry, and leaky bucket.

- If you want to develop successful new product ideas to launch, there are two essential ingredients you need in addition to the FEAST innovation framework. Those ingredients are people and time.

To maximise your success, you need to assemble an innovation team. You should:

- Recruit people from inside and outside your business. Gather a minimum of four people and a maximum of ten.
- Recruit people with different areas of functional expertise, as well as a mix of ages, gender, nationalities and experience levels.
- Aim to recruit yaysayers rather than naysayers.
- Allocate a timeframe to your innovation project. The average time period is about three months.

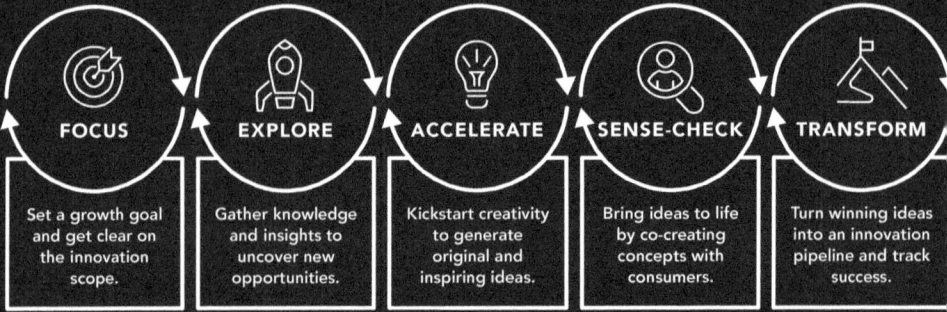

FOCUS

Set a growth goal and get clear on the innovation scope.

EXPLORE

Gather knowledge and insights to uncover new opportunities.

ACCELERATE

Kickstart creativity to generate original and inspiring ideas.

SENSE-CHECK

Bring ideas to life by co-creating concepts with consumers.

TRANSFORM

Turn winning ideas into an innovation pipeline and track success.

you are here

STAGE 1:

Focus

'Effort and courage are not enough without purpose and direction.'

– John F. Kennedy

I recall a time when I was presenting some exciting new biscuit ideas to my management team. I was looking for approval to put the new ideas into full product development. The marketing director was thrilled with the results – so thrilled that she said, 'We should launch them into India too.'

Hear that? That's the sound of the goalposts being moved. It was the first time India had been mentioned.

I checked the original scope of the innovation project. It was for a fast-tracked launch in Australia to fill an urgent sales gap. Adding a new country in parallel would delay this goal.

Once reminded of the original project intent, the marketing director readily agreed that Australia was the priority and gave the approval to proceed. Phew – scope creep averted.

It's scary how quickly scope creep can occur in an innovation project. Scope creep refers to changes, often unintentional or uncontrollable, that occur in relation to a project's focus. It happens most commonly when the project is not properly defined, documented or controlled, and it can feel like the rug is being pulled out from under you.

Whenever you commence a new project, you should always be clear on what you have committed to deliver from the start, and be ready to hold yourself and others accountable for this. While I know you're excited to start developing new products, and your team is raring to go, now is the time to stop and decide what you're going to focus your innovation efforts on. Trust me – doing this early will save you hours of wasted time and debate later.

It also helps to clarify just how far you're willing to stretch as a business for this innovation project, and what it will take to get all your stakeholders in agreement. This stage will ensure you avoid that dreaded scope creep, as well as any awkward 'But I thought you meant' conversations, which could trip you up later.

In Stage 1, I'll show you how to set a product innovation growth goal, and how to match that goal to your innovation scope. You'll also learn how to re-express your innovation challenge, and how to compile a list of innovation ingredients.

Set a Product Innovation Growth Goal

If you give a person a bow and arrow and tell them to shoot, their immediate response will be to ask, 'At what?' In contrast, if you set up a target and ask them to hit the centre, they now have something tangible to aim for. The same rule applies to product innovation – you need to decide on an innovation target to shoot for upfront. Otherwise, how will you know whether your innovation project was successful?

I call this a product innovation growth goal. And it should answer a simple question: How much sales growth do you need from your product innovation?

It's a question that many businesses can't answer.

This is why innovation agencies are let off the hook, time and time again, on what they deliver. Too often, I see businesses sign up with an innovation agency and agree on the delivery of a set number of ideas. 'Sure, we'll find and deliver ten ideas,' the agency agrees gleefully. This means you'll be left holding ten product ideas without any clue as to their value or worth to your business. There are not many other areas of business where this lack of impact or accountability is allowed.

To prevent this from happening, you need to link your product innovation requirements to commercial objectives. Specifically, the amount of sales growth you're aiming for. This shifts the outputs and success measures of your innovation project to the *quality* and *value* of the ideas you create, not just the *quantity* of them.

There are lots of ways to set a sales target for an innovation project. Given that you're aiming to create an innovation feast – whereby you have a menu of new product options that you can browse and select from as your business grows – I'd like you to set a three-year goal. Three years is a great target to aim for as it aligns with most businesses' sales planning horizon. It's also far enough out to give you the time to create truly innovative products to drive sustainable growth.

Here's how you do this:

Step 1: Determine your three-year total business sales growth target. Most businesses have an idea of this, even if they don't have the plans to support it yet. If you don't have long-term business growth targets, now's a good time to change that. Are you aiming for a steady three per cent per annum, or rocketing along at twenty per cent to fifty per cent? Your growth strategy will depend entirely on your category and business aspirations. However, it can be helpful to consider not just your own business's historic performance, but also whether you're performing within growing or declining product categories overall. Category growth rates can be purchased from FMCG retail data providers, like Nielsen or IRI, or you could ask your retail buyer for category growth rates, as they track these and product sales performance regularly.

When setting your three-year business growth targets, some key questions to consider are:

- How fast have you been growing or declining for the past two years?
- Are you trying to outpace the market growth to increase your market share?
- Who is your best performing competitor and can you outperform them?

Step 2: Find out how much of your historic sales came from new products versus current ones. I define 'new products' as anything that was launched in the last three years, because some products require this much time to become established and fully penetrate a market. After three years, these are then counted as your current products. What percentage of sales, and what dollar amount, did each product type contribute annually? Don't worry about whether you're using retail or ex-factory sales – pick whatever is easiest for you to measure and consistently track.

Step 3: Determine the gap between your total business growth and current product sales contribution. Split out your total business growth over three years, and project out the anticipated growth from your current products. Now is the time to consider your other growth levers too, such as organic market growth, new channel expansion, price increases, or increased advertising or promotions. Factor the impact of these growth drivers into your current product performance over the next three years. Now, compare your overall business growth targets for each year with your anticipated current product performance for each year. Do you have a gap between these? If so, this can become your new product innovation growth goal.

It's important to factor in all your other growth drivers as well as product innovation, because these build on your existing business strengths and capabilities and are often less time consuming and risky than new product innovation. As you answer these questions, create a Product Innovation Growth Goal chart to visualise the gap between your current product performance and three-year total business ambition. I've provided a simple example of what this might look like.

Product Innovation Growth Goal
To create a pipeline of new products that will provide sales of $9 million by 2021.

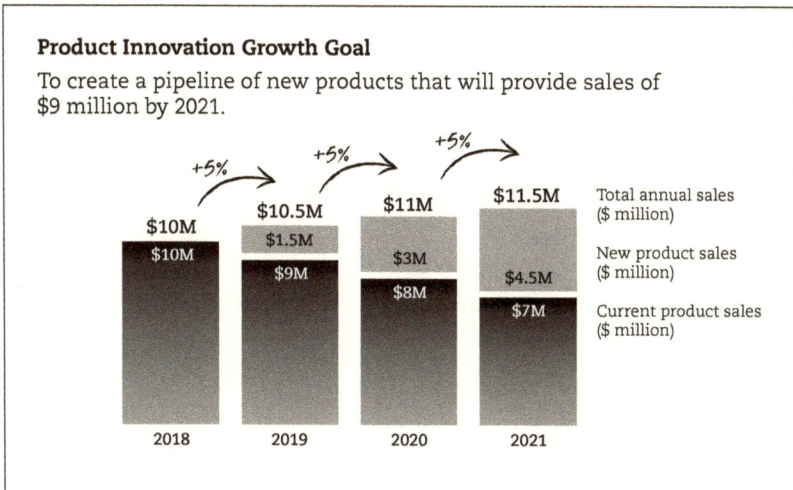

Chart data:
- 2018: +5% — Total $10M ($10M current product sales)
- 2019: +5% — Total $10.5M ($9M current product sales, $1.5M new product sales)
- 2020: +5% — Total $11M ($8M current product sales, $3M new product sales)
- 2021: Total $11.5M ($7M current product sales, $4.5M new product sales)

Legend:
- Total annual sales ($ million)
- New product sales ($ million)
- Current product sales ($ million)

In my example, I'm a producer of unchilled orange juices and have exhausted all my other growth levers in a declining product category. I estimate that my current products will continue to decline by ten per cent annually over the next three years, as retailers cut back on available shelf space and people buy more chilled juices, which they believe to be fresher and healthier. I'm looking to turn around my business trajectory to a healthy five per cent growth per annum in order to keep my business running profitably. Accordingly, I have a sizeable $9 million sales growth gap over the next three years. This is my product innovation growth goal.

By doing this exercise, you're forced to put a clear commercial value on the growth expectations you have of new product innovation. In my example, it's clear that some fairly hefty new product innovation is required to turn this juice business around. A new pineapple-lime flavour extension simply isn't going to cut it. That's why it's not unusual for me to go into a large business and face a sizeable goal, like filling a $50 million sales gap over the next three years. It's critical at this stage for you to understand how much and what impact the product innovation needs to have.

Now you have your three-year product innovation growth goal – an actual sales target for new product innovation. The next step is to ensure this goal aligns with your innovation scope, so that you're able to achieve it.

Match Your Innovation Scope to Your Innovation Goal

'It was so disappointing. It barely lasted six months on the freezer shelf before it was delisted.'

I was told this by the product manager of an ice-cream manufacturer. She explained that a great tasting, new ice cream her business had launched had been delisted after six months due to low sales. The new product was their sixth new flavour variant for the range, presented in the same plastic tub, with the same design, at the same price point, and in the same sales channel as the existing five ice-cream flavours. The business had spent twice as long creating the new product – sourcing the ingredients, developing the recipe, designing the artwork and making the product – than the length of time it had sat on the freezer shelf waiting to be purchased. It hadn't even paid for the time, effort and investment required to make the new flavour.

So, what went wrong? In short, the business used the wrong type of innovation. Why is this problematic? Because not all product innovation is created equal.

Imagine you're on a tennis court and you try hitting a bowling ball over the net. You'd strain and probably break the racket before the ball moved very far. Next you try a basketball. It might bounce over the net, but it's not still ideal for the game of tennis you had in mind. Finally, you try a tennis ball. It's light, small and bouncy, which means you hit it clear over the net and it bounces just right for a return shot. Now you're in the game.

If you want to play a ball sport, you need the right type of ball for the game you want to play. Innovation strategy is exactly the same. In product innovation, you need the right type of innovation for the business result you're after.

THE THREE TYPES OF PRODUCT INNOVATION

Allow me to introduce you to the Innovation Ambition Matrix, created by Bansi Nagji and Geoff Tuff. I use this when businesses want help developing new product ideas, because it helps clarify what type of innovation you think you want, versus what you actually need.

The Innovation Ambition Matrix classifies three different types of innovation, based on how far it stretches from your existing products. It's useful because it focuses on the different degrees of product change, and the resulting risk and rewards that accompany each. As you can see, there are three types of innovation: Core, adjacent and transformational.

Innovation Ambition Matrix

Transformational
Develop new products for new markets & consumers

Adjacent
Expand into 'new to company' markets & consumers

Core
Optimise existing products for current markets & consumers

Markets & consumers — Existing / Incremental / New

Use of products & assets — Existing / Incremental / New

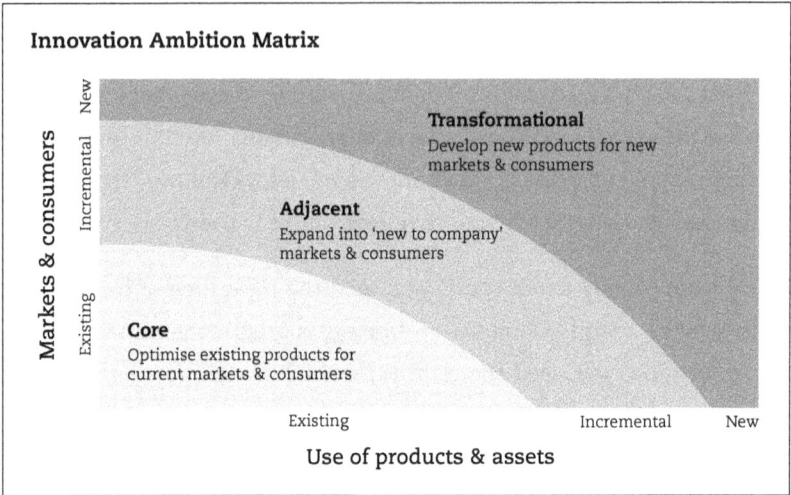

Source: The Innovation Ambition Matrix, Nagji & Tuff, 2012

1. Core Innovation

The first type of innovation, which people are most familiar with, is core innovation, also referred to as renovation. Core innovation is any new changes made to existing products for existing markets or consumers. This includes changes like packaging redesigns, flavour extensions and limited editions.

Core innovation is usually done to make product improvements for your current consumers. For example, Sanitarium, the makers of the much-loved Australian breakfast cereal Weet-Bix, launched a 'Blends' range of Weet-Bix featuring new ingredients such as cranberry and coconut. These products were in the same rectangular product shape, in the same cardboard box, and sat beside the existing range on the supermarket shelf, at a slightly higher price point. The new pack design highlighted the new ingredient blends, thereby offering more variety and flavour interest to consumers.

The role of core innovation is to keep your current business growing steadily and humming along. It's typically low investment because core innovation usually uses assets and capabilities you already have, like manufacturing, supply, sales and branding. And given you're doing what you already know how to do, it's usually low risk.

I am a big fan of core innovation, especially when it comes to new food and beverage products. People are naturally wary of what they put down their throats, and huge, disruptive changes in everyday food items are typically rejected by consumers in favour of familiar products with a small change. I call this the 'same but different' effect.

However, the downside of core innovation is that because these types of smaller, close-in product changes are not really attracting new users or stretching your business into new markets, they offer lower reward in terms of sales return. They often end up reminding loyal consumers to re-purchase their favourite product, or prompting light buyers to repurchase your products again. It's hard to get massive, rapid growth from core innovation. It's more of a slow, steady burn that keeps your existing products relevant and growing in order to fund the riskier, higher return innovation.

If core innovation were a meal, it would be like a regular weekday dinner at home with your family. It's a familiar, tried-and-tested recipe that everyone loves, with a little variation now and again. Maybe a dash of different herbs here, or a new sauce flavour added there, but essentially you're serving up a much-loved meal that will keep the troops happy.

2. Adjacent Innovation

Adjacent innovation requires a greater degree of product innovation. It focuses on creating products that are new and incremental to your business (as opposed to a product category or marketplace), which enable you to enter a new market or reach a new consumer group.

Adjacent innovation opens up larger growth opportunities, but usually requires more investment. In order to appeal to each new market or user, your product may need a greater level of change, so you must invest more to adapt or add to your current capabilities. This could include new packaging or product formulations. For example, Sanitarium launched Weet-Bix Go, a range of breakfast biscuits to be eaten on the go. They feature a new bitesize biscuit shape, in new snack bags at a new price point. The change to a portable format opens up a whole new market for Weet-Bix, appealing to busy people who don't have the time to sit down and eat a bowl of cereal with milk in the mornings, or who want a quick snack between meals.

Adjacent innovation can be terrific for achieving higher sales because it expands your consumer base and product reach. However, as you're focusing on a market or consumer that is less familiar to your business, you also increase the risk of not satisfying them fully, so the risk of market failure increases.

If adjacent innovation were a meal, it would be like going out to dinner at a nice restaurant you haven't visited before. It's new and exciting, and offers food choices you normally wouldn't make for yourself at home. However, it's also a little bit risky, as you hope the meal you've ordered lives up to your expectations and the extra expense of eating out.

3. Transformational Innovation

Transformational innovation – also referred to as disruptive or breakthrough innovation – focuses on creating a new product or market that doesn't exist yet. It has the highest risk and reward profile because you're entering the unknown. There's usually a sizeable investment required to develop a new product that hasn't been offered before, such as new packaging, product formulations or manufacturing equipment. Plus, there's a high risk that you don't understand or aren't able to serve the new market or consumer, so failure rates are high. However, if you are successful, the rewards of transformational innovation can be huge because it unlocks a whole new untapped opportunity for your business.

For example, Sanitarium launched Up&Go, an on-the-go breakfast drink with the protein, energy and fibre of two Weet-Bix and milk in every 250ml serve. This created an entirely new category of liquid breakfast products, and was so well received by consumers that the number of Australians purchasing breakfast drinks more than doubled over the past decade. Up&Go continues to dominate this new market, appealing to time-poor consumers who are eating breakfast on the go, and who previously bought juices, energy drinks, muesli bars or flavoured milks.

Transformational innovation is the sexiest form of innovation – the kind that you read about in business magazines, on blogs or in the news, often with headlines featuring the words 'disruptive change'. However, you should be wary of treating transformational innovation as a silver bullet. It's like cooking a marshmallow with a flame-thrower – it can sometimes be overkill for what you really need.

Transformational innovation is like a fancy meal you enjoy on a really special occasion, such as a twenty-first birthday or a wedding. It doesn't come along often and it's usually very different from something you'd eat every day, as it takes a lot of time, effort and expense to prepare. For this reason, if it's done right, it's really memorable and people will rave about it. However, they'll be equally as unforgiving if it's done wrong.

While you may think it's wise to focus solely on one type of innovation, a balanced approach – which uses all three types of innovation – has been proven to work best. Bansi Nagji and Geoff Tuff reviewed successful innovators in industrial, technology and consumer goods businesses. They found that those who outperformed their competitors opted for a seventy-twenty-ten split with regard to the type of innovation they used. They called this the Golden Ratio.

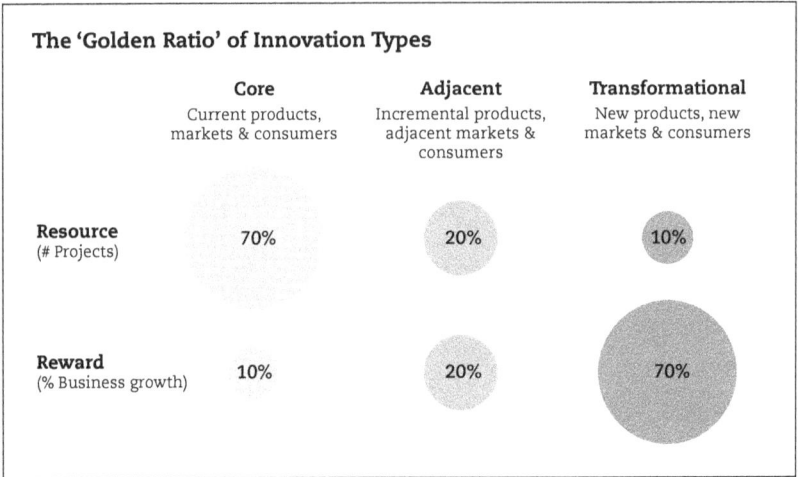

The 'Golden Ratio' of Innovation Types

	Core Current products, markets & consumers	Adjacent Incremental products, adjacent markets & consumers	Transformational New products, new markets & consumers
Resource (# Projects)	70%	20%	10%
Reward (% Business growth)	10%	20%	70%

Source: The Golden Ratio, Nagji & Tuff, 2012

Successful innovators spent seventy per cent of their resources on core innovation, twenty per cent on adjacent innovation and ten per cent on transformational innovation. Yet, in terms of business returns, the reverse proportions were true. These successful businesses balanced short-term predictable growth with longer-term riskier bets, achieving ten per cent of their growth from core innovation, twenty per cent from adjacent innovation and seventy per cent from transformational innovation.

I'm not suggesting you force your innovation plans to fit this ratio, but I wanted to highlight the choices available to you in terms of selecting different types of innovation to drive growth. Every business will have different growth aspirations and a different innovation mix. The reason I am sharing this information with you now is so that you're aware of what type of innovation your business has been using, and why you may have been getting the return you have. This knowledge of innovation types will also help you decide what type of innovation you need to use in the future. This is essential for our next task, which will help you determine what's in and out of scope for your current innovation challenge.

Define Your Innovation Scope

With the three types of innovation in mind, it's time to decide how far and wide you want to go on your innovation journey. Rather than assuming you want transformational innovation or falling back on core innovation, you need to challenge your thinking to ensure your innovation scope will enable your product innovation growth goal. By defining your innovation scope – that is, what you will and won't include in your innovation project – you can ensure you're allowing enough room to get the result you need.

What's in the Pot?

This is a simple exercise to pressure-test what you're willing to include in your innovation project. What's in the Pot helps you determine what's in and out of scope, allowing you to steer clear of the enemy of innovation – project scope creep. Here's how you do it:

Step 1. To get started, grab your innovation team and draw a large circle on a whiteboard or flipchart. Imagine it's a large cooking pot and you're deciding what to put in the pot to make the kind of soup you want.

Step 2. Go through the following questions to help challenge and decide your innovation project scope:

- **Geography**: Where will this innovation go? Which countries, regions, states or towns are to be included?
- **Consumers**: Who are you trying to satisfy? Your current consumers? Or are you willing to reach new ones? This will significantly impact how much growth your project achieves. In addition to identifying potential new customers, are there particular types of customers you *wouldn't* want to make a product for?

- **Product:** Will you go beyond the current products you have? Will you consider different sizes, ingredients, formats, methods of preparation or usage?

- **Brand use:** Will you use current brands or are you willing to create a new one?

- **Packaging:** Will you consider new packaging formats, materials and sizes?

- **Resources:** Who is going to help you with this project? Who will be involved from your business, as well as external suppliers and agencies?

- **Manufacturing:** Will you use processes and equipment you already have? Or are you willing to consider a new manufacturing approach that you don't currently use? This is a real tester. Many businesses want new products but are torn by the need to use their existing manufacturing assets to maximise current capacity and capital investments. This is where it's important to remember your product innovation growth goal. If you need more growth, it's more likely you'll need to make or do something different to what you've done before. This is another good debate to have early within your business. You want to avoid having your project derailed at the end when your supply team says, 'But we can't make that,' and then won't consider different manufacturing solutions.

- **Supply:** Will you source ingredients or finished goods from new suppliers?

- **Pricing:** Will you be open to different pricing models or retail price points?

- **Sales channels:** Will you look at new sales channels? For example, if you develop a product that's designed to be eaten on the go, it might be better off in a vending machine or petrol station than a traditional grocery store.

- **Cost:** What budget do you have to spend on your innovation project in the front-end phase? If you're a small to medium business and willing to do a lot of the stages for yourself, allow yourself a budget of five to ten thousand dollars. This will enable you to buy product samples, hire a venue room, incentivise consumers and fund some basic design sketches – all of which will be needed in later FEAST stages.

- **Time:** In the Warm-up Stage, I asked you to commit to a timeframe in which to complete the five-stage FEAST framework. Three months should be sufficient to complete your innovation project while allowing three to four days per week for other work commitments.

Step 3. Have everyone in your project team write out possible answers to the scoping questions above, and capture these on Post-it notes. Then discuss and review each answer as a team to decide together whether to place it *in* the pot, meaning you will allow it within the project scope, or *out* of the pot, meaning you won't include it. Capture your agreements of what's in and out of scope in a summary like the one shown here.

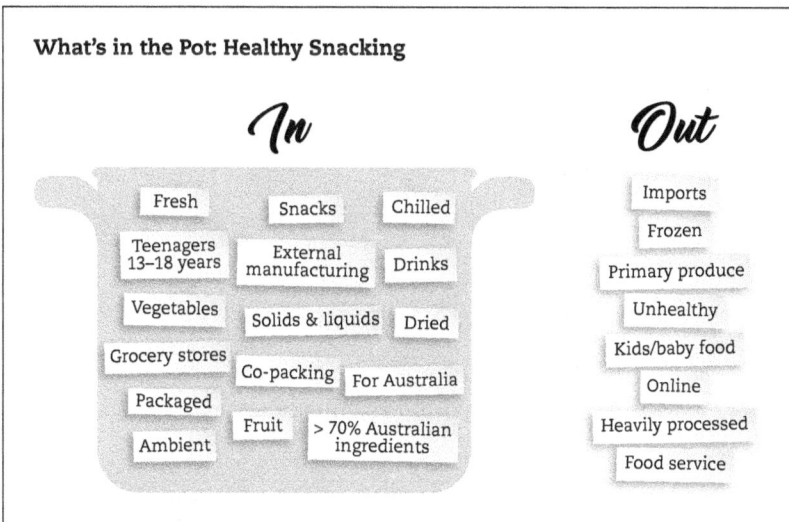

What's in the Pot: Healthy Snacking

In

Fresh	Snacks	Chilled
Teenagers 13–18 years	External manufacturing	Drinks
Vegetables	Solids & liquids	Dried
Grocery stores	Co-packing	For Australia
Packaged		
Ambient	Fruit	> 70% Australian ingredients

Out

- Imports
- Frozen
- Primary produce
- Unhealthy
- Kids/baby food
- Online
- Heavily processed
- Food service

The aim of What's in the Pot is to challenge yourself and your team to consider every possible scoping scenario and whether you'll include it or not. It's much better to have those debates and reach agreements now than realise you had different assumptions later on.

Here's an example of the project scope for a healthy snacking innovation project I worked on. The innovation challenge was to increase market share in healthy snacking among teenagers.

To determine the scope of the project, my team and I decided to focus on the following parameters:

- **Geography:** For Australian consumers only, because we weren't ready for global domination just yet and wanted to ensure success in one market first.
- **Consumers:** For teenagers aged thirteen to eighteen years, not young children or babies, given the strict marketing and food restrictions for those target markets.
- **Product types:**
  - Include mainly Australian grown or sourced ingredients.
  - Be chilled, fresh, ambient, dried or dehydrated, but not frozen because of the expensive and restrictive supply chain issues.
  - Be a snack.
  - Be a solid or liquid.
  - Be processed for long shelf life, rather than raw, unpackaged primary produce.
- **Sales channels:** Be sold in grocery stores, because we wanted a mass-market opportunity.
- **Manufacturing:** Use external contract manufacturing and packaging suppliers.

By clarifying our project scope upfront, my innovation team could immediately focus on where to go looking for new product opportunities, which is vital for Stage 2. We knew even at this early stage that we would focus on Australian consumers who shop in grocery stores, wanting a locally sourced healthy snack. Areas we would explore more broadly included new packaging and product formats. We also knew we'd need to find expertise in manufacturing and packaging, which we didn't currently have access to.

If you've done this exercise right, you will have been forced to answer questions you hadn't thought about, and you'll already have made some tough decisions. You'll also have a sense of whether you'll be able to achieve your innovation goal. Have you given yourself enough scope? If you plan to use the same manufacturing process, the same suppliers, the same sales channel, the same pricing, the same products and the same packaging, in the same geographical region, *and* you're expecting massive sales growth, you will need to think again. If you go down this path, you've already limited yourself to only core innovation with lower returns. If you've agreed to go bigger and wider in scope, you're more likely to go after adjacent and transformational innovation opportunities for higher rewards.

This tool is helpful to keep you on track as you progress through your innovation journey. It's also invaluable to remind other business stakeholders what you agreed to cover at the start, just like I did with the marketing director who wanted the biscuit launch extended to India. I suggest you do this exercise with your innovation team and your manager or senior stakeholders. This will ensure that all your project do-ers and business decision-makers are on the same page from the very beginning.

Once you've made a list of your scope parameters, put it somewhere you can see it throughout your innovation project to remind yourself – and your team – what you agreed on.

Re-Express Your Innovation Challenge

If you're reading this book, chances are that someone in your business asked you to do an innovation project. I call that request an innovation challenge. It's the job to be done. You might receive an innovation challenge that is expressed in a number of different ways:

- Product-centric: 'We need to make different cakes.'
- Category-centric: 'We need to play in the healthy snack category.'
- Consumer-centric: 'We need to recruit young millennials into wine.'

The bigger your business, the more corporate jargon is usually used to express this challenge. I once started on a new innovation project and was puzzled when the brand director told me his objective was to 'increase usage of health-based yellow fats'. I had no idea what he was talking about, but it didn't sound very appealing or motivating. As I asked more questions and he explained the topic, I realised that 'yellow fats' was a retail term for margarine and he wanted to do product innovation on health-based spreads, such as those with cholesterol-lowering benefits. The manager was so ingrained in his business that he didn't call his products by their regular names anymore.

Have you ever been part of a conversation that sounds like death by business jargon? Here's an example of the difference between jargon and normal, everyday language:

Business Jargon: 'There's an increasing incidence of purchase among our target market for our NPD, which is increasing the cannibalisation of our existing portfolio.'

Everyday language: 'People are buying more of our new stuff instead of our old stuff.'

When expressing an innovation challenge, there's an irresistible tendency to use corporate jargon and acronyms to make it sound more credible and business-like. A typical brief reads like this: 'We want to increase our market share in healthy snacking among teenagers.'

Not very motivating, is it? If you want your team to feel inspired to work on your innovation project, I suggest you re-express your innovation challenge in 'real people' speak. Using clearer and more motivating language also helps bring the underlying issue to life. It's not about dressing it up or changing the core problem to be tackled – you're simply expressing it in a new way to prompt a different way of thinking about it, and to gain clarity on your real focus.

Here's how you do it:

Step 1: **With your innovation team,** write down the innovation challenge that was given to you on a flipchart. In my example, the original innovation challenge was to 'Increase market share in healthy snacking among teenagers.'

Step 2: Look at your challenge – brainstorm ideas about what the underlying problem is that you need to solve or the end result you need to achieve. Capture all your responses and select the one that clearly and best captures the underlying job to be done. In my project, my team decided the underlying project objective was to develop a healthy snack that teenagers actually *want* to eat rather than reaching for junk food.

Step 3: On a separate flipchart, write down a list of different people that your innovation task may relate to. It might be the target market or someone around them. In my project, this was people like teenagers, parents, school canteen operators, dieticians and fitness coaches.

Step 4: Now ask everyone in your project team to choose one of these people and answer, 'How would they talk about and solve our innovation challenge?' Put yourselves in their shoes and answer it from their perspective, using their language, expressions and mindset. For example, if I were a teenager, how might I talk about a snack I really wanted to eat? Well, my daughter often comes home from school and says, 'Mum, my friend had this cool new snack in her lunchbox today, can you get me some of those?' So for my snacking challenge, I would capture the expression: 'coolest lunchbox snacks.' Write down all the new language and expressions about your innovation challenge.

Step 5: Now circle the words that best capture the intent of what you're trying to achieve with your innovation project, and the ones that appeal the most to your team. What you're looking for is a more motivating and evocative way to express your challenge. In my project, we decided creating 'the coolest lunchbox snacks' was a more motivating and consumer-led outcome to aim for than 'increase market share'.

Step 6: And, finally, using these statements as inspiration, re-write a more motivating innovation challenge that uses everyday language (not corporate jargon), starting with: 'How can we...' For my project, we ended up with a re-expressed challenge of: 'How can we make the coolest lunchbox snacks for teenagers that taste great and are surprisingly healthy?'

Can you see how a phrase like 'coolest lunchbox snacks' creates more interest than 'increase market share'? Our re-expressed innovation challenge ensures we keep our focus on making a healthy snack, and reminds us how important it is to capture the desire of our teenage consumers. By ditching the jargon and adding some emotive language, you'll have a much more motivating innovation challenge to work on.

Compile an Innovation Ingredient List

This is the final step in clarifying all the inputs and outputs of your innovation project. While you may be tempted to skip this step and not write anything down, it's worth pausing to do this. If you need other stakeholders' approval later on, this tool is invaluable for gaining their buy-in now, as it gives your project an extra layer of clarity and focus. The Innovation Ingredient List acts like a recipe card. It details what you're going to put into the project in order to maximise the success of the new products that come out of it. With your innovation team, fill in each key section of the Innovation Ingredient List, like the example shown below.

Innovation Ingredient List

Name: Project Thrive

Innovation Challenge: How can we make the coolest lunchbox snacks for teenagers that taste great and are surprisingly healthy?

Who:

- Susie - Team leader
- John - Supply Chain
- Phillip - Insights
- Wendy - Sales
- Jennifer - Product Developer
- Project Sponsor - Jane, General Manager

Why:

- Hungry teenagers are busier than ever and seeking high-fat, treat-style foods to fuel up on between meals.
- There's an opportunity to offer healthier snacks to fuel their growing bodies and minds.
- Options needs to be portable, satisfying and nutritious.

When:

- New product launches required for September (pre-summer) in 2019, 2020 and 2021.
- Three-year pipeline proposal due by September 2018 for General Manager's approval.

What:

- Fresh, chilled, dried or dehydrated food and beverage products with more than 70% Australian ingredients.
- Focus on teenagers aged 13–18 years.
- Australian market only, sold in grocery stores.
- Project budget of $20,000.

Win:

Product Innovation growth goal = $5 million of new product sales by 2021.

Here's how you do it:

- **Project name:** Give your project a code name. Stop talking about 'our new corn snack project'. The last thing you want is for competitors to catch wind of what you're doing. Try to keep it a secret for as long as possible by giving it a project name. In my example, I'm calling it Project Thrive, as my team is going to create new healthy snacks that help teenagers feel healthier in their body and mind.

- **Innovation challenge:** Write your re-expressed innovation challenge here. I captured my re-expressed challenge here of: 'How can we make the coolest lunchbox snacks for teenagers that taste great and are surprisingly healthy?'

- **Why**: Why are you doing this innovation project at all? What prompted your business to want to undertake this work? What is currently happening that you want to change or solve? My snacking project is based on the opportunity to satisfy hungry teenagers who are filling up on junk food between meals.

- **Who:** Who is part of your innovation project team? By flagging this now, you'll ensure their managers are aware of, and approve of, their time commitment to this project. Clarify who the project leader is (that's you) and who the end decision-maker is. It's your responsibility to deliver the outcomes, and it's their responsibility to give you the time, resources and approval to proceed at key stages. Who else is helping? Who may hinder you? Who else do you need? Now is the time to ask and clarify these key resource questions.

- **What:** What is your project scope? Write down your What's in the Pot outputs here, and include your project budget. By doing a lot of the FEAST stages myself, and only paying for venue hire, consumer incentives, product samples and basic design work, I've done the whole process for between five and ten thousand dollars. Not a bad investment to create a future product pipeline worth thousands or millions of dollars.

- **When:** How long do you have to complete this project? When do you need to launch something by? When will you need to provide progress updates to your business? In my instance, I need the first new product ready for launch in September 2019.

- **Win:** What does success look like? Write your product innovation growth goal here, and any other deliverables your business has. My goal is to develop $5 million in sales from new products by 2021.

Key Learnings and Actions

Well done, you've completed Stage 1. You should now be crystal clear on what you are trying to achieve with your innovation project. Your goals, success measures, resources and scope have all been determined and agreed on. You are set up for success.

You're now ready to start finding new untapped product innovation opportunities, which we'll discuss in Stage 2. But first, here's a summary of the key learnings and actions from Stage 1.

KEY LEARNINGS

- There are three different types of product innovation – core, adjacent and transformational. Each has a different reward and risk profile.
- Successful innovators focus their business resources on a mix of core innovation (seventy per cent), adjacent innovation (twenty per cent) and transformational innovation (ten per cent) to fuel long-term growth while balancing out their innovation risks and rewards.

KEY ACTIONS

- Go to: **www.eatdrinkinnovate.com.au/if-bonus** and download the free templates to complete your Stage 1 tasks. These include: the Product Innovation Growth Goal, What's in the Pot and the Innovation Ingredient List.

- Set yourself a product innovation growth goal for the next three years. Check that it's reasonable, considering what your business or the market has achieved before. Capture this in the Innovation Growth Goal template.

- Clarify the scope of your innovation project. How far are you willing to stretch your current capabilities to achieve your growth goal? Determine what's in and out of scope before you start. Capture this in the What's in the Pot template.

- Determine all the inputs and outputs of your innovation project. This will clarify what resources you'll use, and when you'll provide new products to your business. Capture this in the Innovation Ingredient List.

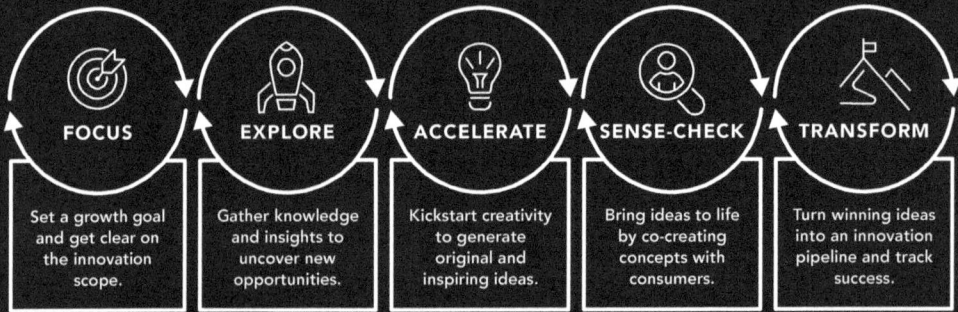

FOCUS

Set a growth goal and get clear on the innovation scope.

EXPLORE

Gather knowledge and insights to uncover new opportunities.

ACCELERATE

Kickstart creativity to generate original and inspiring ideas.

SENSE-CHECK

Bring ideas to life by co-creating concepts with consumers.

TRANSFORM

Turn winning ideas into an innovation pipeline and track success.

you are here

STAGE 2:

Explore

> 'You may feel very secure in the pond that you are in,
> but if you never venture out of it,
> you will never know that there is such a thing as an ocean.'
>
> C. JoyBell C

I was sharing some new dessert ideas with a group of consumers. So far, they'd been very encouraging about the new packaging, ingredients and names proposed. It was time to get into more detail.

'So, what flavours would you like this new dessert to come in?' I asked them.

They looked thoughtful.

'Chocolate.'

'Strawberry.'

'Vanilla.'

'Okay,' I said. 'Those flavours are all available right now. How about something new or different?'

'Um... caramel?'

There are a lot of innovation tools and techniques to help you find new product opportunities. The majority tell you to start by finding out what your consumer needs or wants. However, just like my experience above, there are some things you can't directly ask people. Asking consumers what new products they want is a waste of time.

This is because the majority of people are limited by what they know in the here and now. People struggle to imagine other alternatives and will, therefore, give you close-in, familiar or well-liked product ideas that already exist. If you want innovation that mimics what's already in the market, that's fine. However, be aware that this minimises the likelihood of you creating something truly unique and valued that will be sustainable in the market and secure long-term growth for your business. That's why I believe this is not the best way to find new product opportunities.

What you need to do is uncover the underlying needs, wants, pain points and gain points of your consumers. If you understand these, you can come up with many different solutions to provide products that satisfy them in new ways. To uncover new opportunities, you need to dig deeper than simply asking your consumers what they want. Instead, you have to go on a knowledge hunt – and that's the initial focus of Stage 2. In this stage, I'll introduce you to three do-it-yourself insight-gathering tools, and explain how to create Opportunity Springboards.

Embark on a Knowledge Hunt

Collecting, keeping and sharing knowledge is one of the hardest things to do well in business. People have all this experience and tacit knowledge in their heads or on their computer drive, but it's often hard to access and share widely. When employees leave or change roles, the knowledge often walks out the door with them.

The first thing you need to do is capture what you and your team already know, before you rush out to acquire new knowledge.

Imagine that you're about to go on a hike through the wilderness. You wouldn't just rush out and start randomly pushing through trees and leaping over boulders, would you? Unless you're Bear Grylls, you'd probably do some preparation in advance, like check the weather reports, read some blogs on good camping spots, get some advice from friends, or consult a map to find a good hiking trail.

You may be going into territory that's new to you, but chances are some-one has already blazed a path where you're looking to go. By adopting a common-sense approach and collecting existing knowledge first, you'll save yourself a lot of time and money. You can then decide whether you want to use the existing information or replace and enhance it with your own learnings.

Whether you're collecting new or existing knowledge, it tends to come in three forms: Data, information and insights.

Data is raw numbers that have been captured to represent an agreed standard of measurement. These numbers usually appear in some sort of spreadsheet or table. At most, it tells you what you're looking at. For example, this table shows the milligrams of various vitamins in a single serve of cheddar cheese.

Vitamins	
	Amounts Per Serve
Vitamin A	1323IU
Vitamin C	0.0mg
Vitamin D	15.8IU
Vitamin E (Alpha Tocopherol)	0.4mg
Vitamin K	3.7mcg
Thiamin	0.0mg
Riboflavin	0.5mg
Niacin	0.1mg
Vitamin B6	0.1mg
Folate	23.8mcg
Vitamin B12	1.1mcg
Pantothenic Acid	0.5mg
Choline	21.8mg
Betaine	0.9mg

Source: Nutrition Facts for Cheddar Cheese, Self-Nutrition Data, 2017

Information is a collection of data points that helps you understand something more about what is being measured, such as dates, locations, and any increases or decreases. It's often presented in the form of charts, graphs or summaries, like the one shown here. This chart captures the reduction in export sales of cheese and curd in Australia, from $81 million in December 2016 to $67 million in January 2017.

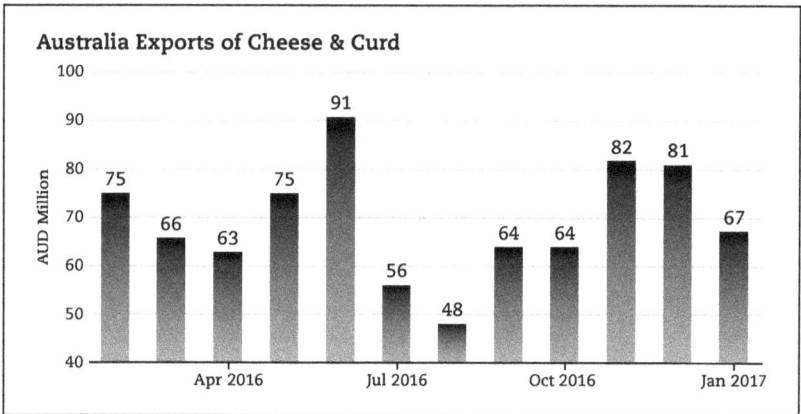

Australia Exports of Cheese & Curd

Source: *Australia Exports of Cheese and Curds, Trading Economics, 2017*

While data and information can provide lots of valuable knowledge, they are often unable to explain causality, or *why* something is happening. Relying only on data and information to infer causality can be misleading, because correlation doesn't equal causality. Just because two incidents follow a similar pattern, that doesn't automatically mean one caused the other. This is clear in the example below, which shows that a statistical correlation exists between cheese consumption and the number of people who die from becoming tangled in bed sheets. Despite the strong correlation, you cannot conclude that eating cheese causes death by bed sheet entanglement!

Per Capita Cheese Consumption
correlates with
Number of People Who Died by Becoming Tangled in Their Bedsheets

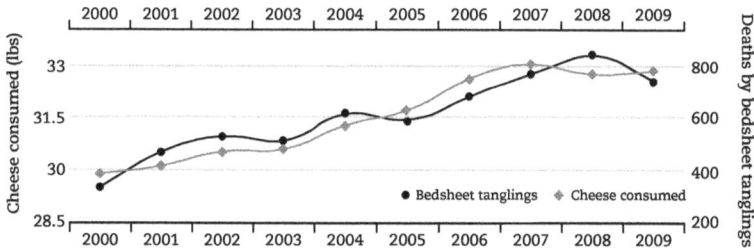

Source: *Spurious Correlations, Tyler Vigen, 2017*

Most businesses are rich in data and information. They have lots of reassuring facts and figures about their sales, market share, pricing and growth rates. However, they tend to lack meaningful and actionable insights.

Insights explain *why* a particular behaviour, situation or phenomenon is occurring. These usually reflect people's underlying needs, wants, attitudes, motivations and perceptions. For example, just imagine you found out that fifteen per cent of households with children bought cheese snacks in the last month, compared to just five per cent of households without children. You have enough data and information to know that, for some reason, parents with kids are buying more cheese snacks than people without children, but you don't know why – you're missing an insight here.

By interviewing parents who buy cheese snacks, you would discover that they believe cheese snacks are a healthier way to fill up hungry kids between meals than handing out sweet biscuits, potato chips or muesli bars. However, they're irritated that young children can't tear open the sealed wrappers themselves. What a wealth of insights you now have. Understanding *why* parents are buying cheese snacks, and what else they *need* from these products, opens up a treasure-trove of new product opportunities. Now you can create the ultimate single-serve, ready-to-go cheese snack in an easy-open pack that young children can rip open themselves.

This is why uncovering insights is a must-do for product innovators, because it drives a consumer-centred mindset. In other words, insights encourage you to put your consumer needs at the heart of everything you do. And the best product solutions come out of the best consumer insights.

Together, data, information and insights provide knowledge.

GATHER YOUR EXISTING KNOWLEDGE

To collect data, information and insights, let's start your knowledge hunt by gathering what you already know. The first exploration exercise is called Fast Blast. The aim is to capture and reveal as much existing knowledge as possible. This will expose knowledge gaps, so you can then focus on acquiring that new knowledge. Here's how you do it:

FAST BLAST

Grab your innovation team and as quickly as you can, write down in bullet points everything you already know about your innovation challenge. Try answering the knowledge-gathering questions below about the category, consumer and capabilities you're interested in. Don't make assumptions, guesses or hypotheses. Capture real facts, data and insights only.

Fast Blast knowledge-gathering questions:

CATEGORY:

- **Performance:** Is the market growing or declining? How crowded is it with competitors? Who's established and dominant on shelf?

- **Products:** What types are already available? How much new product innovation is there? How much shelf space is there in-store?

- **Brand:** Who is competing in the market? How are they positioned?

- **Sales channel:** Which channels are products sold through? What other channels could be used?

- **Geography:** Where are products sold? How are products distributed or shipped?

- **Costs:** What are the prices in-market? What are the profit margins?

- **Legal and regulatory:** Are there any legal or regulatory requirements or restrictions?

CONSUMER:

- **Shopper:** Who is the buyer? What's motivates or detracts them?

- **End user:** Who's consuming these products? Why, when and how are they using these products? Remember that your user may not be the same person as the shopper. For example, if a mother purchases a lunchbox snack for her child, the mother is the shopper and the end user is the child.

- **Functional:** How, where and when is the product used?

- **Emotional:** What needs or wants does the product satisfy?

CAPABILITY:

- **Formulations:** What ingredients are used? What product claims do they make? For example, no preservatives, low-GI, and so on.

- **Supply:** Who supplies raw materials, formulations and packaging?

- **Manufacturing:** How are products made? When? Where? Why?

- **Promotion:** How are products advertised and promoted?

- **Packaging:** How are they packaged? What design imagery and features are used?

Capture what your team already knows by placing each piece of knowledge on a Post-it-note and putting it into the following Knowledge Hunt Summary.

Knowledge Hunt Summary

	What we know	What we don't know
Consumer		
Category		
Capability		

DIVE DEEP INTO NEW KNOWLEDGE

Now that you have a better understanding of what your innovation team already knows, let's go deeper and broader by doing a Deep Dive to find out what other people and businesses in the marketplace also know. Here's how you do it:

DEEP DIVE

With your innovation team, brainstorm a list of other people, businesses and resources who may have knowledge about your innovation challenge. Look inside and outside your own business. Your goal is to identify these knowledge holders and learn everything they know through interviewing and research.

There are bound to be lots of people inside and outside your business who have untapped experience and knowledge relevant to your innovation project. These people and their expertise are a goldmine you need to tap into and capture. They may be the veteran in the factory, the young apprentice or the agency hotshot.

When preparing to speak with people, keep your opening request simple. I like to start with a phone call or email, worded like this:

> 'Hello Sandra, I'm working on a project to come up with new product ideas for healthy snacks. I'd be really interested in talking to you to understand what you know about that topic. Could you spare thirty minutes to chat with me this week?'

Not many people refuse the opportunity to share their expertise and insights. If they do, simply try someone else. You can cover quite a lot of ground in thirty minutes of interviewing, especially since you won't be doing much talking at all. Spend your time wisely, by probing deeply and soaking up all the information that these people know. Use the list of knowledge-gathering questions to help frame what you will ask. Obviously, tailor your questions once you identify exactly which area your interviewee has knowledge of. For example, the factory manager may know a lot about the capability side of things, how products are made, what's been tried before, and who the best material suppliers are in the market. However, he may not know about the pricing and promotion of competitor products, so focus your questions accordingly.

Don't forget to seek written information too, such as market trend reports, industry magazines, blogs, podcasts and news reports. Check that your list of people and resources will give you good coverage across the three key knowledge areas: consumer, category and capability. Your aim is for each team member to speak with at least three people and review three written resources. If you have between four to ten members on your innovation project team, this will give you more than enough new knowledge on these three priority areas.

Once you've come up with a list of people to interview and resources to collect, divide these up among your project team equally, and agree to meet back in two weeks to compile and share your knowledge. This is a good timeframe to keep your project momentum going and enable you enough time to gather new knowledge.

Once you've done this, gather all your learnings and add them to your Knowledge Hunt Summary. Now is the time to grab your team and review together what you *do* know and still *don't* know. Where are your big gaps? What are you still missing? This will direct you as to where you need to spend more time and effort to fill in these knowledge gaps. This is the point where a lot of innovation teams realise they've collected lots of data and information about a category or product, but not many underlying insights about why things are that way. For example, remember our cheese-snack-buying parents from earlier on? You may find out that of all the cheese-snacking children, those aged ten to fourteen years are consuming the most, but you're still not sure why that is – are they simply the hungriest, or are there other factors at play? Don't worry – I have some great tools to help you get these missing insights in the next section.

GET CLOSER TO YOUR CONSUMERS

You should now be clear on your knowledge gaps. In order to fill in those gaps, you need to gain some insights. Now, you could enlist a research agency to do this for you, if you have the funds. This is a good way to save time and your personal effort, plus you get a pretty neat-looking report at the end of it all. However, it takes much longer, is more expensive, and you're usually kept at arm's length from real consumers. At best, you may end up watching them through a two-way mirror in a research room, as though you and they are both dangerous substances that shouldn't be mixed.

It's so much more worthwhile doing this exercise yourself. Your concerns about lack of research finesse and interviewing expertise will be overcome by the amazing eureka-like 'Aha!' moment when you uncover an insight for yourself. It's incredibly powerful and liberating. For example, imagine you see a tired working mother hurry home, unpack the kids and groceries, and quickly thrust a cheese-stick at her hungry child. You personally experience the insight of 'I need something fast, easy and nutritious to tide my kids over until I can get dinner ready.' Reading that as printed words in a report simply doesn't compare with seeing, hearing and capturing this insight yourself.

With that in mind, it's time to grab your adventure gear and head off the well-beaten path. This means going where no one, especially your competitors, has gone before to find fresh, untapped insights and opportunities.

Uncovering insights is the secret to staying ahead of your competitors, finding fresh new opportunities, and creating new products that are meaningful and successful. It's all about understanding *why* you're creating something. How can you possibly create a new product for someone if you don't know what they want and why they want it? This is where many product innovators fall down. They assume they know what their customers want, not realising they need to check this frequently throughout the entire new product development process.

Now, remember that most consumers are terrible at telling you what they want. But they can tell you *why* they do what they do, and this is where you'll find valuable insights. If you understand why people want or need something, you can make many different products that satisfy them in a new way.

I never cease to be surprised at the knowledge gems you pick up by seeing how, when and why people use certain products. I stood in a kitchen once, watching a woman swing open her fridge door to get out a bottle of salad dressing. It was one of many glass bottles, balancing precariously, upside down, in the fridge door shelf. When she reached in and took out one bottle, the rest toppled over and banged against each other. She explained sheepishly, 'I have to store them like that. Otherwise I can't get the last bit out of the bottle.'

What a huge opportunity for product improvement that simple observation and insight offered! I could make the dressing runnier so it flowed more easily out of the bottle. I could introduce a plastic squeezy bottle. I could create an upside-down bottle with a wide base. I could create a plastic tub that thick dressings could be scooped out of... the possibilities were endless.

So, who should you approach to gain these insights? Before you rush out to speak to everyone, use the Consumer Immersion Wheel to help direct who to talk to. This tool gives you guidance on some of the people it would be worth spending time with to gather insights from.

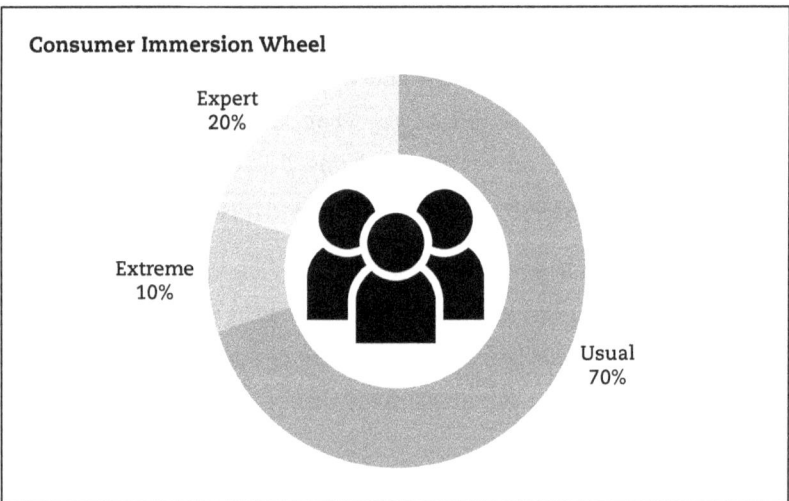

Consumer Immersion Wheel

Expert
20%

Extreme
10%

Usual
70%

There are three types of people I think you should approach: Usual, expert and extreme consumers.

- **Usual:** Usual consumers are regular people who have a direct connection with the product areas you're most interested in. They are the usual users or consumers of the product type or category you're exploring. Your goal is to understand why they buy and consume what they currently do. Going back to my healthy snacks example from Stage 1, usual users would include teenagers who regularly eat snacks. The goal would be to find out what types of food and drink they choose and why.

- **Expert:** Expert consumers are people who have an indirect and in-depth connection to your innovation challenge. They're not the users or consumers, but influencers, experts or opinion leaders in the area you're interested in. In the context of my healthy snacks innovation challenge, I might talk with people who are knowledgeable about health issues, such as dieticians, nutritionists, health food stores and gym instructors.

- **Extreme:** Extreme consumers have a stronger relationship (either positive or negative) with your area of interest. You're looking for people who have a stronger connection than the average person. They may be die-hard fans or die-hard haters. For my healthy snacks project, I may talk to marathon runners, people with eating disorders or fast-food junkies to understand their unique and extreme perspectives on healthy food.

To achieve a good balance of consumers to talk to, I suggest seventy per cent of your time be spent with usual consumers – their opinion counts the most after all. Then twenty per cent of your time with expert consumers – your goal is to look for extra gems of opportunity that regular consumers might not even realise they need or want. And, finally, spend ten per cent of your time with extreme consumers. Although they're generally the most fascinating and challenging, you can get irrelevant or misleading insights here, so treat them as the extra spice or salt you add to flavour a meal – not the main ingredients.

The entire purpose of approaching these three different types of people is for you to uncover the reasons behind their behaviour, choices and preferences. With your team, create a list of who you're going to talk to in all three consumer groups. Remember, the purpose is to engage with real people for yourselves. Before you go and talk to anyone, however, you need to adopt some insight-ready behaviours.

TWO ESSENTIAL INSIGHT-READY BEHAVIOURS

Imagine you're watching a family eat some salsa dip with corn chips. You see a ten-year-old boy re-dip the same corn chip in the bowl three or four times. No one else seems to mind, but you wince noticeably as he happily continues to double dip. Immediately, the family is reminded that you're watching them. Mum belatedly scolds her son for bad manners and they all eat very carefully after that. All those juicy opportunities to observe their true behaviour, and potentially create the ultimate double-dip-free corn chip, are lost.

This is the first behaviour to adopt when you're observing people – **be neutral and don't judge**. Avoiding verbal and nonverbal judgement is essential when talking to and observing consumers. You want to uncover real opportunities, like how to prevent double-dipping, that only arise when you witness true behaviour and attitudes. This also means avoiding invasive or judgemental questions, like: Why do you eat so much between meals? Allow people the time and space to show and explain their own choices. Remember, you're not the focus – they are.

Nonverbal signals of judgement can be just as powerful as verbal ones. I have to stop myself from nodding when I hear something that I agree with, to avoid inadvertently leading people's responses. So, as hard as it might be, you must look, sound and act neutrally when talking with people.

The second behaviour is about curiosity – **don't assume anything!** If you genuinely don't know anything about a category, user or topic, then researching it becomes so much easier because you're a blank canvas waiting to be filled. However, if you've worked in a particular product category for a while, there's a tendency to assume you know everything about it. You may find it harder to step back and adopt a naive, child-like approach to exploring. You'll be full of prior knowledge, experience, theories and assumptions, and may subconsciously filter your observations to support these. This is called confirmation bias. To overcome this, you need to adopt an attitude of professional naivety. It's helpful to imagine you have to explain what you saw and heard to an alien who has just landed on Earth and knows nothing.

Now that you know how to behave in an insight-ready fashion, let's dive into some handy tools that you can use yourself.

Do-It-Yourself Insight-Gathering Tools

To get great insights, you need to use qualitative questioning techniques that uncover people's attitudes, perceptions and motivations. The benefit of this type of research is that it's great for exploring new and unknown things.

But what if you feel nervous about how to approach and speak to your consumers? Don't worry. The insight-gathering tools I'm about to share with you are easy and effective ways to connect with people, and they don't require you to be a research guru.

There are three insight-gathering tools that are easy to use and will help you capture valuable insights into your consumers:

1. Interviewing with TED.
2. A Day in the Life.
3. Shopper Safari.

These can all be used on usual, expert and extreme users. Ideally, these techniques would be undertaken by two people. This is because it's easier if one person asks the questions, while the other person observes and captures people's responses. If you can't find someone to help you, try to film or record your insight immersions instead. Recordings can be invaluable later – to share with stakeholders when you need to demonstrate the fresh opportunities you've uncovered.

1. Interviewing with TED

The most direct way to gain insights is to interview people. Invite them into a neutral space either individually, in pairs or in small groups, depending on your confidence when it comes to interviewing multiple people at once. Don't be tempted to save time and effort by talking with fifteen people in one group at the same time. That's like trying to cook using every hotplate – it's noisy, chaotic and you can't focus on one thing properly, so everything ends up burnt or boiling over. To give people sufficient time and space to contribute fully, I suggest you interview no more than six people in a group at one time. I usually prefer to work with pairs or groups of three. People tend to be reassured by the presence of others and it's not as intense as a one-on-one interview. Plus, you can generate some great discussions as people share their different perspectives and preferences.

The quality of people's responses depends on the quality of the questions you ask. So, your goal here is to ask open-ended questions that encourage expansive, storytelling answers. These responses are usually jam-packed with helpful insights into why people do what they do. The death of any interview is when you're met with constant yes/no or one-word responses. To avoid this happening, the TED interviewing technique is an effective tool to use. It is used by call centres, business coaches and even the police force. TED can guide you to phrase your questions in a way that prompts open-ended, storytelling responses.

TED suggests you include three key words – tell, explain and describe – in your interviewing questions. All these words encourage insight-rich, explanatory answers. It's virtually impossible to answer a TED question with a single word.

Here's an example of an interview *not* using TED questions, about people's beverage choices for breakfast, especially tea and coffee consumption:

Question: What did you have for breakfast today?

Answer: Cereal with milk and a cup of tea.

Question: What sort of tea?

Answer: English Breakfast

Question: Why did you have that particular tea?

Answer: I like the taste of it.

Failing to incorporate TED questions makes the interview as difficult as squeezing blood from a stone. By using TED questions, this interview becomes much more insightful:

Question: Could you please **describe** what your breakfast was like this morning?

Answer: It was pretty rushed. I have to get to work by 8am, so I just had some cornflakes with skim milk and a cup of tea. It's not the healthiest choice but it's easy to make and eat quickly.

Question: Can you **tell** me more about the types of tea you like?

Answer: I only ever drink English Breakfast from a teabag with milk and sugar, because it's mild-tasting and sets me up for the day. Then I'll have a coffee when I'm at work.

Question: Could you **explain** the difference between having a tea compared to a coffee?

Answer: I really want a tea when I first wake up and at the end of the day after dinner. It's warm, comforting and it's my little moment of calm. I usually prefer a coffee mid-morning or mid-afternoon because it gives me a boost to get going.

See how much richer the responses become when using the TED interviewing technique? Each response opens up new areas that you can probe and dive into. It's much better than asking people outright, 'Why do you…?' Over-use of the word 'why' can make some people quite defensive. After all, you are asking them to explain themselves in a very direct way, which can sound like an implied judgement. Because of this, you usually end up with very rational, sensible and socially responsible answers. This may be miles away from the highly irrational, emotional and spontaneous reasons that really lie behind the behaviour you're exploring.

Here's a simple running guide to help you structure your interviews with consumers:

Step 1: Introduce yourself.

Step 2: Explain broadly what you'll be talking about with them. For example, in my tea and coffee research, I'd say, 'Today, we're going to be talking about what you eat and drink for breakfast.'

Step 3: Build rapport and put your interviewee at ease by firstly asking questions they're familiar with, before asking about broader concepts. Then narrow down on specific topics of interest. Remember to use the TED questions to encourage storytelling about what they do, and don't forget to probe into how they feel too.

- **Start familiar**: Ask about what they do currently. For example, what they currently eat for breakfast, how it's prepared, where it's bought, or how family members differ in their food and beverage choices.

- **Go broad:** Ask about bigger, future-based concepts that they may not think about on a daily basis. For example, challenges in food preparation or quality, importance of family meals together, or concerns over nutrition and healthy eating at breakfast.

- **Be specific:** Probe deeper into the specific areas of interest around your innovation challenge. For example, tea versus coffee consumption in the morning, types purchased, and perceived differences in benefits and limitations.

Step 4: Thank them for their time and responses, and end the interview.

It's a good idea to prepare some questions in advance so you can easily refer to them as needed. This way, you'll stay on-track and ensure you don't miss any important topics. These questions will vary greatly depending on your innovation project focus, so just remember to cover off the big areas of interest: *What* are they doing? *When* are they doing it? *How* are they doing it? *Why* are they doing it? And, most importantly, how do they *feel* about it?

To capture your interviewees' responses, I like to use an Insight Capture Map, which is a version of an empathy map, first created by design-thinking innovators at IDEO. This map helps you capture the different types of responses you may hear or see during your interview.

Insight Capture Map

Say	Think
Do	**Feel**

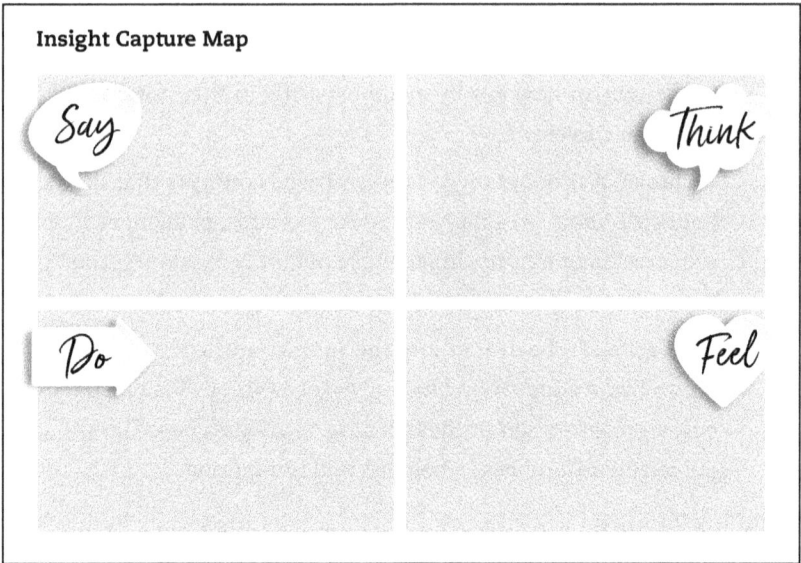

The Insight Capture Map has four key quadrants that you fill in during your interview:

- **Say:** What are some quotes and key words the person said?
- **Do:** What actions and behaviours do they do?
- **Think:** What are they thinking? What does this tell you about their attitudes, motivations and preferences?
- **Feel:** What emotions are they feeling?

2. A Day in the Life

The power of this second insight immersion tool is its use of observation in situ. You're going to step into your consumer's world and spend time with them as they undertake a task or use a product of interest. The aim is to take photos, capture stories and quotes, and write down all the actions you see, as well as the way people describe things. This will give you plenty of insights into how people act, feel and think, as well as their problems, their unmet needs and their moments of satisfaction.

To capture your observations and insights, I like to use a Day in the Life Map. This helps you capture not just the actions a person takes, but also their emotional responses, such as:

- **Pain points:** Things that annoy them.
- **Gain points:** Things that give them real satisfaction and joy.
- **Wish points:** Things that are missing, which they really want.

Here's an example of a Day in the Life Map, showing the actions and healthy snack choices of a teenager named Jess. It also shows her pain points, gain points and wish points:

Day in the Life Map

	Jess				
Do	Home from gym & hungry	Picks veggies from own garden	Chops into small cubes	Makes own salad dressing	Single serve, stores rest in fridge
Say	'I've got to eat healthy after that work out'	'I love growing my own veggies'	'So I can eat it quickly with just a fork'	'I make the same one every time'	'It's worth the effort'
Think	'I hate having to prepare food'	'Only way I trust they are fresh'	'Isn't there a machine that does this?'	'I'd like to have a few more dressing options'	'What a relief – that's tomorrow's lunch sorted'
Feel	Pain	Wish	Pain	Wish	Gain

Here's how you do it:

> **Step 1:** In your consumer's environment (this may be their home, office or even car), ask them to undertake a particular task or use a product of interest, in the same way they did the last time they used or consumed it.

Step 2: As they're doing this, observe what they do, and ask them to explain what they're doing and why. This will help you identify their motivations, concerns and preferences.

Step 3: Ask questions *only* to clarify and expand on their responses, not to lead or judge them. For example, I would ask Jess, 'Tell me more about the types of salad dressings you like making,' rather than saying, 'It must be boring to always make the same salad dressing. Wouldn't you like more variety?'

Step 4: Gather all your observation notes and fill in the Day in the Life Map.

As shown in the example above, let's imagine you're standing with Jess, a health-conscious eighteen year old, aiming to find out about her healthy snacking habits. You watch her as she returns home from the gym and decides to prepare a salad to snack on. She picks vegetables from her Mum's garden, makes her own salad dressing, and serves herself a bowl of salad. While she does this, you ask her to explain every action she takes and the reason she's doing it. Why did she choose a salad to make? Why does her Mum grow her own vegetables? How does she feel about preparing the salad? What does she wish was easier, faster or better? The fresh and unique insights you can uncover that underlie people's behaviour and choices are endless.

If your consumer is completing a short, one-off event, such as making a salad, then it will be easy for you to observe and map the whole experience. However, if it's a long or ongoing event, like using a slow cooker over eight hours, you may want to watch key parts of the event (such as preparing the ingredients), and then ask the consumer to simply talk you through the rest of their intended actions.

Repeat this exercise with a few consumers, and you'll start to see major themes and patterns occurring. These may be surprising reactions, shortcuts or work-arounds. For example, you might discover how much Jess hates cutting up vegetables, or how she makes two servings of salad to keep one for the following day and how she likes picking her own veggies so she doesn't have to visit the grocery shop every day. These observations represent unmet consumer needs, pains or gains, which can all serve as inspiration for new product innovation ideas.

3. Shopper Safari

This final insight-gathering tool is used *where* products are purchased, and it's called a Shopper Safari. Like a Day in the Life, this is an observational immersion exercise that reveals the impact of a store environment on a shopper's behaviour and choices.

The difference between this exercise and A Day in the Life is that you're seeking to understand what drives shopping choice, rather than product use or consumption. In Shopper Safari, you're observing in-store what is capturing consumers' attention, what's prompting their selections and purchases, what irritates or confuses them, and how a product's appearance on shelf influences them.

Here's how you do it:

Step 1: Accompany a shopper on their purchasing trip for a particular product or category of interest. The objective here is to see what impact the store environment has on your consumers' actions. For example, I would accompany Jess on a salad-shopping mission. I already know that she uses some of her own grown veggies, but I've learnt that she also does a regular shop for fresh ingredients that aren't grown at home.

Step 2: Follow your shopper as they walk through the store, and ask them to talk about what they're doing, thinking and feeling as they make purchase choices. For example, as I'm walking beside Jess in her local grocery store, I see her pick up a large, raw beetroot and pause, before putting it down and moving further down the aisle to select a vacuum-sealed pack of smaller, peeled beetroots. I ask her about her choice and she explains that she loves beetroot in her salads, but hates peeling the raw ones. They're too big, messy to handle, and usually dry out before she eats the whole thing. She prefers the packet of ready-peeled, mini beetroots, as they're still fresh and much easier for her to cut up and use one at a time. She's happy about the time and hassle this saves her.

Step 3: Using an Insight Capture Map, write down your observations on what your consumer says, does, thinks and feels as they shop. For example, I would write down in 'Do' that Jess chose the ready-peeled and sealed beetroot pack over the raw beetroot. I'd capture her exact words about the mess and inconvenience of raw beetroots. I'd write down how she 'feels' happy that she's saving herself time and effort, and that she 'thinks' the pre-peeled, sealed beetroots are just as fresh as the raw ones.

Shopper Safari – Insight Capture Map

Say
'I hate peeling and chopping those big, raw beetroots. They stain my hands and chopping board, plus I can't eat it all before it dries out.'

Think
'I think the pre-peeled and sealed packs are just as fresh as the raw beetroot.'

Do
I saw Jess pick up a raw beetroot, then put it down and select a sealed pack of four small, pre-peeled beetroots instead.

Jess

Feel
Jess feels happy that she's saving herself time and effort without compromising on the freshness of the beetroot.

Once you've used all three insight-gathering tools, take a moment to reflect. Are you surprised by the quantity of new actionable insights and fresh knowledge you now have?

The final critical step of Stage 2 is to review all the knowledge that your innovation team has collected from your three insight immersion exercises: TED Interviewing, Day in the Life and Shopper Safari. Share and review your Insight Capture Maps and Day in the Life Maps together. Collate all the new insights from these and add them to your Knowledge Hunt Summary under 'What We Know'.

Now, take a moment to pause and check. Do you feel you have enough knowledge to help tackle your innovation challenge? Here are a couple of key questions to consider to help answer that:

- Are you beginning to understand the category, consumer and capabilities around your innovation challenge a lot better?
- Are you already inspired and thinking up lots of new product opportunities?

If the answer to either question is no, you may need to do more exploring and knowledge hunting. If you answered yes to both questions, you're up to the final step of Stage 2. It's time to turn all this knowledge into new opportunities to innovate on.

Create Opportunity Springboards

Have you seen the trampolines available for kids today? They've got these amazingly high and flexible safety nets that wrap the whole way around the base jump mat to prevent kids from falling out or bouncing over the sides. These nets still let kids jump super-high, but keep them firmly within the safe bouncing zone. This is a far cry from the open trampoline I used as a child. One wrong double bounce and you'd be sent hurtling over the edge or onto the skin-pinching springs.

Why am I telling you this? Because trampolines are a lot like Opportunity Springboards, which bring together all the data, information and insights you've collected on your Knowledge Hunt to create a springboard to generate new product ideas from. Just like a trampoline, Opportunity Springboards need to be super springy to help stretch your thinking further. And, just like the trampoline safety nets of today, Opportunity Springboards must also act as a guardrail, to keep you from going completely off-course into undesirable areas.

Here's an example of one Opportunity Springboard for my healthy snacking project.

Veggie Snack Attack

Why:
I want to eat more vegetables to be healthier but I'm so busy and it's such a hassle to peel, cut and prepare them. Also, I don't really know what to make, so I can snack on them during the day.

Who:
Health-conscious teenagers, aged 13–18 years, who want to eat more healthily between meals.

When & where:
Everyday snacking, such as at school, in home and on the go.

Innovation Opportunity:
Offer fresh, delicious and convenient vegetables that teenagers can more easily snack on.

What:
Maintain the high nutritional value, increase the convenience and long-life of fresh vegetables. On-the-go and minimal preparation products. New formats for traditional and trendy vegetables. Replacement for snacking products such as biscuits, bread, crackers and chips.

'I want to eat more vegetables but when they're raw they're really boring.'

'I'm not a vegan but I eat vegan food because it seems healthier to me.'

'Vegetable chips aren't really healthy, but they're better than traditional chips.'

'I always buy heaps of fresh vegetables and end up throwing a lot away because I don't have time to cut, peel and prepare them.'

Here's how you create this:

Step 1. Innovation Opportunity: This is the name and summary of the product, industry or consumer need you're going to focus on. With your team, review your Insight Capture Maps, Day in the Life Maps, and Knowledge Hunt Summary. Circle and pull out recurring needs, wants, pain points, gain points or wishes from your insight immersions. These represent untapped, powerful opportunities to better satisfy consumers, and become the basis for different Opportunity Springboards. Give each Innovation Opportunity a short, catchy name and brief description which is easy to understand and motivating to solve. I often use catchphrases, movie titles, song titles or memes as sources of naming inspiration. In my example, remember how much Jess hated cutting and preparing her salad ingredients? And how she preferred to buy easy-to-prepare alternatives like pre-peeled beetroots? I captured this opportunity as 'Veggie Snack Attack' and gave a short summary of what I meant by this: *'Offer fresh, delicious and convenient vegetables that teenagers can more easily snack on.'*

Step 2. Why: This is your desired consumers' most pressing need, want, pain-point or wish. It must be grounded in the real world and true insights, not something you've assumed or made up retrospectively. Direct consumer quotes and summaries work best here. In my example, I included some of the direct quotes I heard Jess say, which really helped summarise this unmet opportunity, such as: 'I want to eat more vegetables to be healthier, but I'm so busy and it's such a hassle to peel, cut and prepare them.' You can include more than one quote here – just be mindful not to pack this section full of conflicting or competing insights. If I'd included a quote from Jess like: 'I wish I could eat more healthily when I'm driving into work,' that's a completely different insight. It reflects an unmet need for more portable healthy snacks, which would be worth creating a new Opportunity Springboard for.

Step 3. Who: This details who wants or needs this opportunity. The secret here is to capture a meaningful representation of your target consumer. It's more actionable if you describe them according to their attitude, behaviour or need, rather than just demographic features. For example, if I describe people like Jess as 'teenagers aged thirteen to eighteen years old', you gain a fairly limited view of who my target consumer is. Whereas if I extend that to include her attitude to food – 'health-conscious teenagers who want to eat more healthily between meals' – it starts to become clearer that more convenient healthy snacks would satisfy this target consumer.

Step 4. When and Where: This describes when and where the target consumer might experience this opportunity. In my example, I've written everyday snacking, in home and on-the-go. These might be the same or different for each springboard you create, depending on who it is aimed at and why.

Step 5. What: What must the product or experience look like in order to deliver on this opportunity? Try to fill this section with guiding principles about what consumers are looking for. Go back with your team and consult your Insight Capture Maps and Day in the Life Maps. What are consumers doing, choosing, buying or using to fill their needs currently and what gaps remain unsatisfied? These are best expressed as a call to action, so they start directing you towards product ideas. My example includes things like maintaining high nutritional value, and new formats for traditional or trendy vegetables. These are not solutions, so hold back on your desire to start putting new product ideas in here.

Opportunity Springboards need to be evocative, powerful and distinctive areas that are different from each other. I consider them sufficiently 'springy' if they prompt you to immediately start thinking of new product ideas. If you're not sure whether your springboard is on track, ask yourself these questions:

- Does this springboard link closely back to your innovation challenge?
- Is the 'why' compelling? Does it inspire you to understand it and motivate you to solve it?
- Is the 'what' actionable? Does it immediately start prompting new product ideas?
- Would it stretch your thinking versus what's available now?
- Does it make you want to work on it?

You should be aiming to create around three or four Opportunity Springboards per innovation challenge. If you do this exercise and find that you have more than four Opportunity Springboards, then your innovation scope may be too wide and you're trying to tackle too much at once. This makes your innovation task overwhelming, especially when it comes to generating new product ideas using each Springboard. If this happens, divide your innovation challenge into smaller, more manageable projects.

Alternatively, you may have a lot of Opportunity Springboards that are very similar or too narrow in focus. In that case, try combining a few insights to come up with one bigger opportunity. For example, if I had one springboard about consumers' desire for organically grown vegetables and another springboard for vegetables with a known source of origin, I might combine these two insights under a broader 'Nature's Best' springboard and include the need for organically grown and locally sourced fresh produce in the 'What' section.

Key Learnings and Actions

Now that you've identified and defined the new opportunity areas you should focus on, it's time to take your Opportunity Springboards and start ideating. This is the focus of Stage 3. But first, here's a summary of the key learnings and actions from Stage 2.

KEY LEARNINGS

- To undertake a Knowledge Hunt, you need to capture your existing knowledge first. There are three types of knowledge:
    - Data: Raw numbers that represent an agreed standard of measurement.
    - Information: A collection of data points that helps you understand something more about what is being measured.
    - Insights: Explanations that tell you why a particular behaviour, situation or phenomenon is occurring. Uncovering insights is a must-do for product innovators, because it drives a consumer-centred mindset.
- To be insight-ready, you need to ensure you don't judge or make assumptions when talking to your consumers.
- The Consumer Immersion Wheel provides inspiration about who to talk with to gain new insights.
- Three useful insight-gathering exercises you can do with your innovation team are: Interviewing with TED, A Day in the Life, and Shopper Safari.
- The Insight Capture Map, Day in the Life Map and Knowledge Hunt Summary templates will help you capture and collate your data, information and insights.
- Opportunity Springboards capture untapped consumer needs, wants, wishes, and pain or gain points that represent new opportunity areas, which you can create new product ideas from.

KEY ACTIONS

- Go to: **www.eatdrinkinnovate.com.au/if-bonus** and download the free templates to complete your Stage 2 Explore tasks. These include: the Knowledge Hunt Summary, Insight Capture Map, Day in the Life Map and Opportunity Springboard.

- Undertake your Knowledge Hunt using the Fast Blast and Deep Dive exercises to find out what you already know and what else you need to find out.

- Use the Consumer Immersion Wheel to create a list of people you will talk with to gain fresh insights. They may be Usual, Expert or Extreme consumers.

- Undertake insight-gathering interviews using the TED interview technique.

- Undertake insight immersions with your consumers as they use or consume products, and shoppers as they buy products. Capture your observations using the Insight Capture Map and Day in the Life Map.

- Using the key themes from your Knowledge Hunt, create three to four Opportunity Springboards in preparation for the next stage of idea generation.

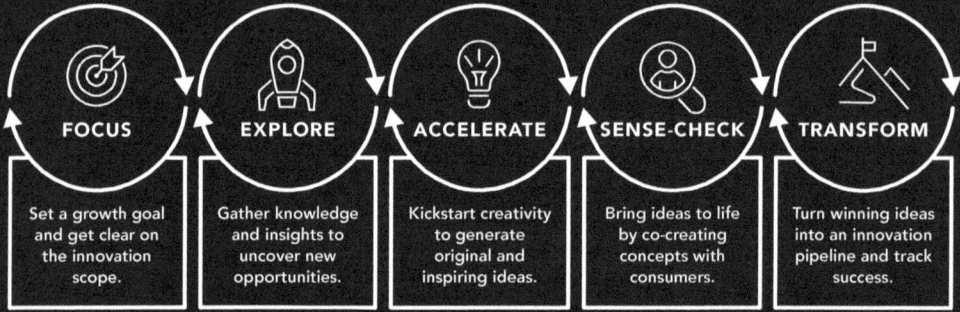

FOCUS
Set a growth goal and get clear on the innovation scope.

EXPLORE
Gather knowledge and insights to uncover new opportunities.

ACCELERATE
Kickstart creativity to generate original and inspiring ideas.

SENSE-CHECK
Bring ideas to life by co-creating concepts with consumers.

TRANSFORM
Turn winning ideas into an innovation pipeline and track success.

you are here

STAGE 3:

Accelerate

'Creativity is giving yourself permission to see things differently.'
– David Robert

I was presenting a new deodorant idea to a leadership team.

'We know that young women want fresh underarms *and* hair-free under-arms. So, the idea is to develop the first ever hair-removing deodorant. Women could stay fresh, dry and hair-free at the same time...'

I had barely finished my sentence when a product development manager tersely cut in.

'Combining the two chemicals required to block perspiration and enable hair-removal would cause serious bodily harm. It can't be done.'

My request to just explore what might be possible was denied. Fast-forward twelve months, a beauty-care competitor launched a hair-minimising underarm deodorant and body moisturiser range. They were the category bestsellers of the year.

Have you ever had a really bad idea? How did you know it was bad?

When I ask this question in workshops or training groups, almost everyone puts up their hand and cringes at a personal memory, very similar to mine. They recall a time when their new idea died a painfully swift, public and premature death.

But have you also had a brilliant idea, which may have seemed bad or impossible at the time and then became the 'big one' that got away? After talking yourself out of it, perhaps you saw it on a shelf, or a friend recommended it to you, or it received retailer awards. Understandably, you felt frustrated – that could have been *your* product!

The only difference is that the people who launched the bestselling, award-winning product didn't kill an 'impossible' idea early. On the contrary, they nurtured it, developed it, and turned it into something feasible and amazing. That's what this stage of the FEAST framework will teach you – how to kickstart your creative thinking to generate fresh and inspiring ideas. I'll introduce you to four creative hacks, show you how to turn your thoughts into ideas, and teach you how to run an ideation workshop to spark original ideas.

Unlock Your Creative Thinking

I like to think of new product ideas as newborn babies. They require a lot of care before they become fully functioning. Can you imagine seeing a friend's newborn baby for the first time, and instantly dismissing its future potential based on its current state?

'Sorry to break it to you, Kate, but she's clearly not CEO material. I mean she can't even sit up, so how is she going to chair board meetings?'

Ridiculous, right? But this is how most people treat new ideas. They don't look for future potential; they look for immediate perfection. They're extremely intolerant of incomplete ideas. They expect them to be commercially robust, clearly defined and ready for implementation the minute they're proposed.

You need to generate messy, incomplete ideas first, so that they can mature and grow into robust, logical and commercially sound ideas. Just like newborn babies, you've got to give them the time and resources to grow into something magnificent without dismissing them too early. You can do this by shifting from critical thinking to creative thinking.

The tendency to critique, and look for the underlying weakness of an idea, is an example of critical thinking. In business, we love critical thinking because it's rational, linear and precise. It's so satisfying when there is a clear right versus wrong, strength and weakness, or pro and con. Most of our formal schooling and work experience has encouraged us to adopt this style of critical thought. And while critical thinking is invaluable to run an effective, profit-generating business, it's the worst thing possible when it comes to idea generation because it kills newborn ideas too early.

To create and nurture really fresh and unique ideas, you need to unlock creative thinking. Here's the difference between the two:

CRITICAL THINKING	CREATIVE THINKING
• Rational	• Curious
• Analytical	• Expansive
• Logical	• Experimental
• Linear	• Divergent
• Precise	• Non-judgemental
• Selective	• Generative

You're thinking critically when you:

- Rely on reason rather than emotion.
- Require evidence.
- See things in black and white.
- Are concerned more with finding the best explanation than asking questions.
- Are precise, meticulous, comprehensive and exhaustive.

You're thinking creatively when you:

- Imagine familiar things in a new light.
- Dig below the surface to find previously undetected patterns and connections.
- Display a great deal of curiosity and are constantly asking questions.
- Are uninhibited in expressing your opinions and ideas.
- Exhibit intellectual playfulness.

Creative thinking is the key to coming up with new ideas because it allows your thoughts to go where most people's thoughts never do. The great news is that you can shift between the two different modes of thought. You just need to warm up your brain first.

Ask a room full of people whether they're creative and about twenty per cent will raise their hand. This is because most people assume being creative means having artistic ability, instead of being able to think differently. For the purpose of product innovation, I'm defining creativity as the ability to generate new and original ideas.

According to a study on the effectiveness of brainstorming, by Terry Connolly, Robert L. Routhieaux and Sherry K. Schneider at the University of Arizona, idea originality is the key to innovation success. So, the real goal of any idea-generating session is to develop not just a large quantity of ideas, but also highly original ideas.

A way to visualise this is by using the Idea Creativity Spectrum. This spectrum works on two dimensions for generating ideas. One is the level of speculation you undertake, or how far your thinking stretches (Y-axis). The other is how original the ideas generated are (X-axis). The more speculative your thinking, the more likely you are to create ideas that are original.

Idea Creativity Spectrum

```
Level of speculation ↑
                          Creative
                          thinking

              Critical
              thinking
                                                    →
              Potential for original ideas
```

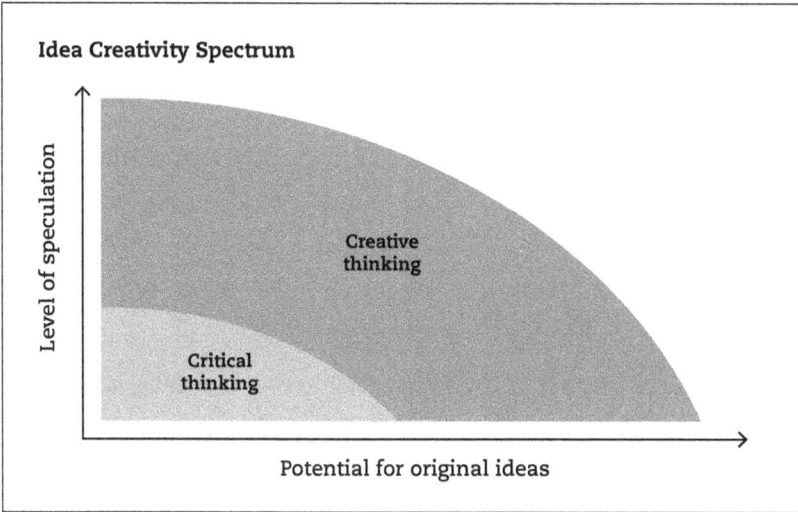

In the following section, I'll show you how to move up the Idea Creativity Spectrum using a series of creative hacks.

Four Creative Hacks You Need to Do

People often protest that they cannot come up with new ideas. They think only geniuses like William Shakespeare, Marie Curie and Pablo Picasso are truly creative. But that's simply not true, because everyone can think creatively. A creativity study by psychologists Connolly, Routhieaux and Schneider suggested that original ideas are generated by using a systematic and structured approach, rather than random brainstorming.

I'm going to introduce you to four effective creative hacks that will prompt you to systematically think differently and help you to create new ideas. A hack is simply a shortcut that makes things easier and faster. Creative hacks are thinking tasks that help you switch from critical to creative thinking very quickly, and move you along the Idea Creativity Spectrum. Making fresh connections is an underlying principle of all these techniques. Creative hacks push you beyond your automatic thinking response and force you to consciously make new connections.

These creative hacks are sometimes referred to as large-scale creativity tools, because they help you generate a large quantity of ideas quickly by considering a range of different perspectives. The four hacks I will share with you are ones that I frequently use because of their distinctiveness and effectiveness. They're my variations on techniques from The Thinker's Toolbox, by Pamela and David Thornburg.

The secret of these exercises is that they have a low-entry threshold, meaning anyone can do them without expert skills or experience. They also have a high-reach threshold, meaning they enable your thinking to stretch broadly. Use these creative hacks in the order recommended to warm up your mind and move up the Idea Creativity Spectrum.

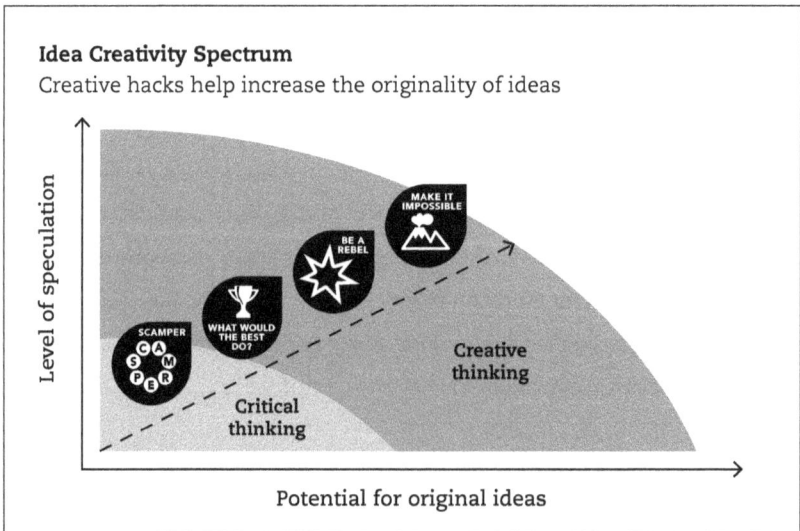

Idea Creativity Spectrum
Creative hacks help increase the originality of ideas

1. SCAMPER

SCAMPER is a tried and trusted creative hack, originally created by Alex Osborne, and further developed into an ideation tool by Bob Eberle. It is one of the most popular and well-known creativity hacks due to its simplicity and ability to generate a large range of ideas from an existing product.

SCAMPER is based on the idea that everything new is a modification of something that already exists. Each letter of the SCAMPER acronym represents a different question to help change or adapt the elements of an existing product.

This is the easiest of the creative hacks because it deals with what you already know. It typically generates ideas that are still quite familiar or close in to what's already in market, such as core or adjacent innovation.

Here's how you do it:

- **Think about an existing product. This could be one that you want to improve, a competitor product you covet, or a product that you think could be a good starting point for your innovation challenge.**
- **Then, answer the following questions to come up with as many new product ideas as you can.**
  - **SUBSTITUTE: What could you take *out* or put *in* to make something new?**
  - **COMBINE: What could you add to make it more unique or valued?**
  - **ADAPT: How could you change what it normally is or does? Consider the way it's consumed, how it's made, how it's packaged or sold.**
  - **MODIFY: Could you magnify (emphasise) or minify (reduce) what it normally is, does or is made up of?**
  - **PURPOSE: What else could you use it for?**
  - **ELIMINATE: What could you remove or delete?**
  - **REVERSE: What could you re-order? The way it's made, sold, packed?**

Let's imagine I am a nut grower who is trying to come up with ideas for new products that use nuts. Here's an example of how I could use SCAMPER and capture the outputs:

SCAMPER

Substitute	• Replace potato in chips with nuts: nut chips. • Add cereal: nut cereals. • Add bread: gourmet nut loaves.
Combine	• Combine with coffee: nut lattes. • Combine with milk: nut smoothies
Adapt	• Blend it: cashew milk. • Grind it into a powder & use as an alternative to wheat flour.
Modify	• Maximise health benefits: nut vitamins.
Purpose	• Make into clothing fibre, like hemp. • Pulp it to make paper. • Mix with grains for vegan pet food.
Eliminate	• Sell in bulk, no packaging – bring your own reusable container & weigh amount you need.
Reverse	• Sell nut bushes. • Pick your own nut plantation. • Self-blend your own nuts.

Once you complete the SCAMPER hack, you've already started moving up the Idea Creativity Spectrum and gone beyond those ho-hum product ideas usually generated in brainstorming sessions. It's important to capture each idea as it comes – don't filter or sense-check them yet. Accept everything. At this stage, you're aiming for quantity and originality. There'll be plenty of time to make these ideas feasible later.

With that in mind, let's move on to the second creative hack.

2. WHAT WOULD THE BEST DO?

This creative hack prompts you to think outside your current product category. It encourages you to consider best-in-class examples from entirely different industries, and make fresh connections back to your own innovation challenge.

Here's how you do it:

- **On a piece of paper, draw three columns.**
- **Write the headings: 'The Best at (*your challenge*)', 'How They Do It' and 'New Ideas' in each column.**
- **In the first column, write down all companies, brands, people or products that are the best at what you want to achieve or solve in your innovation challenge.**
- **In the next column, write how they do it.**
- **Use the 'How They Do It' list as inspiration to generate new product ideas in the third column.**

What you're looking to do here is make connections with other categories and leverage how they are solving a similar challenge. You're not creating a direct copy of their solution.

Let's imagine I'm still a nut grower, but now I want to make a nut-based snack. So, I list some of the best foods or drinks that are doing well in the snacking category, such as the Delicious Chocolate Bar (yes, I made this brand up – you'll obviously use real brands, products or businesses). My first step is to write down everything I know about this product, including the way it looks, feels and smells, how it is packaged, how it is eaten, and the ingredients it contains. Then I use all these details as jumping-off points to inspire new product ideas for nut-based snacks.

Here's what my workings for this creative hack would look like:

What Would the Best Do?

THE BEST AT *snacking*	HOW THEY DO IT	NEW IDEAS
• The Delicious Chocolate Bar	• Chocolate outside. • Soft & hard centres inside. • In a 50g bar format. • Have shiny foil wrapper. • Can eat on the go with one hand.	• Different nut coatings - yoghurt, chocolate, salty seasonings, candy coated. • Dessert nuts – soft, nut-flavoured centres. • Nut tubes, can tip straight into mouth.

The secret with this creative hack is not to be too literal in your jump from what 'the best' in the business currently do to what *you* might do with your new product. For example, just because the Delicious Chocolate Bar is coated in chocolate, doesn't mean your new product idea should be a direct copy, like chocolate-coated nuts. Instead, take the broader principle of 'adding a coating' to come up with something new, like yoghurt-coated nuts, candy-coated nuts, chilli-coated nuts, and so on. By applying the principles of what the best snacking products, brands or businesses are doing, you will end up with many new product ideas, rather than just one direct copy.

3. BE A REBEL

This creativity hack can make you feel uncomfortable because it challenges everything you know about your current products, market or category. This is a good thing. Creative thinking is often about feeling 'comfortably lost' in order to arrive at an unknown destination. Be a Rebel is used to encourage you to actively reverse the known status quo about a certain product or category.

Here's how you do it:

BE A REBEL

- Draw three columns on a piece of paper and add the headings: 'Rules of (your challenge)', 'Break Them' and 'New Ideas'.

- Write down everything about your innovation challenge as it currently exists. In other words, the 'rules' by which the products or category operate. For example, milk must be stored in a fridge.

- Under 'Break Them', write down all the ways you could be a rebel and do the opposite of what the rules are. For example, long-life milk that doesn't need refrigeration.

- Use the 'Break Them' list as inspiration to come up with new ideas in the third column.

For my nut-based snack challenge, my creative hack workings would look like this:

Be a Rebel

RULES OF *nuts*	BREAK THEM	NEW IDEAS
• Hard & crunchy.	• Make them soft or liquid.	• Nut soups, nut purees, nut jelly, nut juice.
• Small, fit in your hand.	• Make them big.	• Grow palm-sized nuts.
• Round or oval shaped.	• Change their shape.	• Add edible glitter, rainbow-coloured nuts.
• Brown or white colour.	• Make them colourful.	• Carve into mini-sculptures or shapes.
• Store in cupboard at room temperature.	• Cook them.	• Give them to animals to eat.
• People eat them.	• Refrigerate or freeze them.	• Make into frozen ice-cream, icy poles or yoghurt.
• Usually savoury taste.	• Make them sweet.	

The hardest part of this exercise is getting from the broken rules to new product ideas. The new ideas are still often radical and impossible. That's okay. For now, challenge yourself and your innovation team to be as free-thinking and unconstrained as possible. We'll make these product ideas more feasible later on.

4. MAKE IT IMPOSSIBLE

If you've worked through all three of the previous creative hacks, you'll be ready for this fourth and final one that takes you to the far edges of the Idea Creativity Spectrum.

Make It Impossible encourages you to create things that are virtually impossible to implement, and then make them possible. The beauty of this creative hack is that it removes all the barriers that stop you from doing something truly disruptive and breakthrough. It's the equivalent of asking that liberating question: What would you do if I guaranteed you'd be successful at it? Make It Impossible dares you to dream big and look for ways to solve what initially seems unsolvable.

Here's how you do it:

- Draw three columns on a piece of paper and add the headings: 'No constraints on (your challenge)', 'Impossible Ideas' and 'Possible Ideas'.
- Now imagine you live in a world with no constraints. Come up with new ideas that would:
  - Be illegal.
  - Be too expensive.
  - Be extremely risky.
  - Be impossible to physically do.
  - Make you a laughing stock.
  - Use things that you can't access or store.
- Write these ideas in the 'Impossible Ideas' column and use them as inspiration to come up with possible ideas in the third column.

Once you've captured these impossible suggestions, turn them into new product ideas that could be possible.

For my nut-based challenge, my creative hack workings would look like this:

Make it Impossible

NO CONSTRAINTS *on nuts*	IMPOSIBLE IDEAS	POSSIBLE IDEAS
• Make them addictive & illegal to sell. • Make them as expensive as precious jewels.	• Nuts coated with drugs. • Gold and diamond coated nuts.	• Snack nuts coated with caffeine and guarana for a natural boost, or vitamins as health supplements. • Nuts coated with edible gold flakes as a premium gift.

In my example, I've decided to make nuts addictive, which is a pretty risky approach that I wouldn't normally consider. An impossible idea based on this would be to coat nuts with illegal drugs like cocaine, so people would keep buying them. I would definitely be jailed for selling these products! Now I tone down the principle of my impossible idea to make it more permissible. This is when I take the underlying principle of 'substances that people crave' and replace the harmful, illegal drugs with something familiar, beneficial and legal, like caffeine or multivitamins. From a shocking start, I've arrived at an idea for nut-based vitamin supplements that give a natural daily boost.

The last part of this creative hack is critical to reining your impossible ideas back in so they are a little more feasible, but still not ordinary. Your aim is to make the impossible possible without losing all the originality.

Turn Your Thoughts into Ideas

Once you've completed these creative hacks, you'll now have many different ideas listed in the various worksheet columns. However, I'm going to suggest those aren't actually ideas yet – they're thoughts. The difference between an idea and a thought is that you can do something with an idea. It's more specific and actionable than a thought.

Let me give you an example. If I phoned my husband and said, 'Hi honey, let's order some takeaway,' this is a thought. His response would probably be a barrage of questions, like: Do you mean for dinner tonight? What sort would you like? Which place shall we order it from? Do you want me to pick it up? What time should I get it?

A thought leaves people guessing about what you really mean, whereas an idea is more specific and actionable. So, instead, I would say, 'Hi honey, let's get Thai takeaway for dinner tonight. If I phone The Golden Palace at 7pm, could you pick it up on your way home from work?'

Now, that's an idea. My husband has enough details to build, adapt or change specific elements of my idea. For example, he might suggest we get Chinese instead, or explain that he'll only be able to pick it up at 7.30pm.

When you're doing the creative hacks and generating so many thoughts, you need to take the time after each exercise to convert your thoughts into more tangible and actionable ideas. The best way to do that is to write up your ideas on a Product Idea page.

I prefer the simple template shown here because it provides enough detail for you to understand and remember your product ideas later on. Avoid the temptation to add lots of executional details at this stage like pricing, packaging or sales return. When you're in the midst of a fast-paced ideation workshop, the last thing you want to do is slow people down with impossibly specific details they can't provide at this stage.

Product Idea

Idea name: Protein-rich Nut Smoothies

What is it?
Range of protein-rich, creamy, thick smoothies, made from organic nuts, Greek yoghurt, honey and seasonal fruits

What makes this exciting?
Liquid breakfast option.
Nuts offer a natural protein boost to start the day.

Who is it for?
Time-poor, health-conscious people wanting a natural boost to start the day.

Here's how you fill in each part:

1. **Idea name.** Make this a short, clear, descriptive name. At this stage, people should be able to understand what the idea is simply by the name.

2. **What is it?** In one or two sentences, describe your idea. This might include things like what it's made of, its ingredients or flavours, and its shape or size.

3. **What makes this exciting?** Describe why you think this is unique, different or worth doing.

4. **Who is it for?** Don't get too tricky. If it's specific to a certain age group or gender, then call it out.

5. **What does it look like?** No matter how limited your drawing skills are, you must draw a picture. It honestly is worth a thousand words and brings the idea to life. It also forces you convey the size, shape, look or feel of the new product that you have in mind.

At the end of an ideation workshop, you're aiming to have between eighty to one hundred Product Idea pages stuck up on the walls. This is when you realise the benefit of a catchy name, brief description and picture. It helps you immediately recall every product idea, and enables you to identify how each may be nurtured, expanded and adapted further.

Run an Ideation Workshop to Spark Original Ideas

Imagine walking into a meeting room and being asked to whip up a gourmet lunch for all the employees in your business. You're handed a cup of flour, a bowl of water and given thirty minutes to complete the request. How would you feel? Overwhelmed? Anxious? As though you're in the wrong place with the wrong tools to complete the task?

That is how most people feel when they step into a meeting room on a regular work day and are asked to 'brainstorm' new product ideas on the spot. They're being set up to fail from the start.

Remember the critical versus creative thinking mindset we discussed earlier? One of the best ways to encourage creative thinking is to run an ideation workshop, specifically designed to generate fresh and original ideas. This means dedicating a set time, in an offsite location, with creative exercises and stimuli to prompt creative thinking. Idea generation is not 'business as usual' and cannot be treated as such. Running an ideation workshop ensures you gather the right people and resources together and put them in the optimal environment to create new ideas.

To ensure you run a productive ideation workshop, there are a few simple elements to get right. Firstly, let's talk about the roles and responsibilities of attendees. Every ideation workshop should have:

- **A project leader:** This is your role. As project leader, you will explain the reason for the ideation workshop, remind people of the Opportunity Springboards your innovation team created, and explain the desired outcome of the session (lots of original ideas!). You get to actively participate in the creative idea-generation hacks too.

- **A facilitator:** This is someone who is great at managing time and guiding people. The facilitator runs the session according to the agreed time and structure, which is set by the project leader. They encourage people to contribute and manage group dynamics, but do not participate in the idea-generating hacks themselves. This is a great role for someone within your business, or a willing external business partner or supplier, who is a natural master of ceremonies – someone that people listen to. They don't necessarily need to know the creative hacks (you'll be able to explain these), but they must be able to control and chivvy along a crowd.

- **Group of attendees:** These people are from your innovation project team, plus a few more inspired thinkers you can rope in for the session. This is the perfect time to go find more of those yaysayers from Stage 1 who are open-minded and love finding new ways of doing things. Their role is to complete the creative hacks and generate ideas. Ideally, no more than twenty people and no fewer than five should attend your ideation workshop. Fewer than five means you lack the diversity and sheer volume of creative input to create enough ideas, while any more than twenty makes crowd control tricky.

Once you've assigned roles and responsibilities to attendees, it's time to run the workshop. To help you get the most out of every single session, there are four ideation energisers I'd like to introduce you to.

FOUR IDEATION ENERGISERS

Have you ever been to a brainstorming session where the person running it reads through a list of bullet points, outlining how they want you to behave for the day? The list might look like this:

- Be creative.
- Listen to others.
- Think outside the box.

This is like showing a group of alcoholics a sign that says 'Stop drinking' and considering the rehabilitation job done. There's no way that's going to work. The likelihood of anyone changing their behaviour just by being told to is extremely low. Instead, it's worth taking the time to model the behaviour you'd like people to adopt, so they learn by doing.

Before you start any idea-generation, you must first encourage and train people to adopt idea-nurturing behaviour. Creative energisers are a great way to do this. These are action-based exercises that help people model and practise desired behaviours. Forget all those nasty exercises which require you to count up in multiples of seven or answer trivia questions at speed. Those sorts of exercises only make people feel stupid and stressed.

The right type of creative energisers are those that set a positive mindset for the day, lay out the ground rules, and model the desired behaviours for the session. They are also intellectually playful and stimulating, which is another key requirement for unlocking creativity. I'm going to share with you four of my favourite creative energisers, which I regularly use in ideation workshops.

1. 'Yes But, Yes And'

'Yes, and...' is one of the most valuable phrases in idea-creation. It was first widely used in improvisational comedy to encourage comedians to build on each others' quips and running gags. Since then, it's been used in a range of diverse settings, from the boardroom to the bedroom, to assist with shared communication, conflict resolution and relationship building.

This energiser demonstrates and teaches you how to build and nurture ideas. It also coaches people on the language you'd like them to use throughout your ideation workshop when responding to other people's ideas.

Here's how you do it:

Step 1: Ask attendees to find a partner to work with. Choose who will be Person A and Person B.

Step 2: Person A is going to share an idea about how to make work more fun. Person B will respond by saying, 'Yes, but...' and then tell them why that idea won't work.

Step 3: Person A will share another idea. Person B will say, 'Yes, but...' and give them another reason why that new idea wouldn't work either.

Step 4: Repeat this exchange three times.

At the end of this exercise, ask both people how they felt during the exercise. Person B usually enjoyed themselves immensely. Why? Because they felt smart and in control. They were the logical and rational one, pointing out all the reasons why Person A's new ideas wouldn't work.

In an everyday business environment, this type of behaviour would be applauded and rewarded. However, in an idea-generation session, it's the opposite of what you need, because Person A is left feeling demotivated and frustrated. Why bother offering new ideas that are just going to be shot down every time?

'Yes, but...' is a passive-aggressive way of saying no. There's no true agreement in the response at all. The 'but' negates everything said before it, signalling the start of premature idea-killing. This behaviour must be avoided in an idea-generating session. It only takes one or two people to criticise ideas early before everyone stops offering them.

Now get your attendees to try something different:

Step 1: This time, ask Person B to pitch ideas about how to make work more fun.

Step 2: Person A must reply with, 'Yes, *and*...' They must build and expand on the new idea to make it better. Even if they loathe the idea, they must find a way to re-direct, build on, enlarge or improve it. Don't worry if the idea changes direction or shape. If it does, all the better.

Step 3: Person B is to then reply, 'Yes, *and*...' and offer suggestions that build on Person A's revised idea.

Step 4: Keep taking it in turns to say, 'Yes, and...' so that each person replies at least three times.

What happened this time? How did people feel at the end of it? Chances are both people felt great, because their ideas were accepted and expanded on, rather than shut down instantly.

When I do this exercise with different groups, the energy in the room is amazing. The noise volume and laughter grows, and people become really animated. At the end of it, the attendees can't recall which ideas belonged to Person A and which ideas belonged to Person B. Because they both contributed, they both feel like the final idea is theirs. Also, the final idea has become much bigger and better than the first idea that was proposed. That's the power of idea-nurturing behaviour. It creates really powerful ideas, which people feel personally vested in and are motivated to make happen.

In idea-generating workshops, you must encourage people to build, not tear down, new ideas. It can be excruciatingly hard to be positive and improve something you don't like or understand. However, by encouraging people to harness their intellectual power and replace 'Yes, but' with

'Yes, and', you and your team are much better positioned to create ideas that are original and amazing.

2. Say My Name

Idea generation is a team sport. The secret of effective idea generation is to approach it with everyone's contribution being equally relevant and valued. If you're dealing with a very hierarchical or functionally divided group, you need to establish equality. This enables everyone to contribute openly without the risk of being shot down or trumped by someone more senior or more experienced.

Doing a quick, energising exercise like Say My Name helps to strip away roles and responsibilities in a humorous way and create an equal playing field.

Here's how you do it:

Step 1: Give every attendee two name labels. On one label, ask everyone to write their full name, job title, and length of employment with their business.

Step 2: Walk around the room, but instead of asking people to introduce themselves, ask them to rip their name label in half and throw it in the bin you're carrying around. Since people were preparing to tell you all about their role and experience, this will create a sense of shock. This is absolutely necessary – you've got to disrupt and shake up the status quo.

Step 3: Now ask them to write on their second label. This time they must write the name of their first pet, followed by the name of the first street they lived on as a child.

Step 4: Now go around the room and ask each person to introduce themselves by their new name. Remind people that their functional roles and responsibilities will not be needed and can, therefore, be set aside for the day.

This activity is hilarious and liberating. It's not based on skill, experience or personal preferences. In fact, it eliminates any sort of bias, judgement or hierarchy, since most people didn't choose their first pet's name or the street they lived on as a child. I did this exercise once with a group of employees which included a director and a very quiet, newly joined graduate. When the finance director introduced himself in good humour as Fluffy Harris, the change in the room dynamic was immediate. The graduate (aka Lady Shuffleton) joined in the general banter and started contributing more fully to the following discussions. As people explain what their first pet was or where they used to live, a lot of sharing happens. It's incredibly humanising, as functional roles and seniority melt away, to be replaced by regular people. It's rewarding to see who emerges as wildly creative once the constraints of hierarchy and functional roles are removed.

3. Treasure Hunt

It's helpful to remind people at the start of an idea-generating session that you want to tap into everyone's unique perspectives and experiences. Treasure Hunt is a great energiser to get to know everyone and build trust quickly. I picked this exercise up from my daughter's school, and have used it in business workshops, university lectures and corporate team-building events.

Here's how you do it:

Step 1: In a big, open space, ask all attendees to stand around so they can hear you. Shout out topics and ask the attendees to quickly find people who are similar to them on this topic, and have them stand together in a group. For example, if you shout out, 'Your favourite sport to play,' people have to yell out the sport they most like to play and find other people with the same passion. Encourage lots of movement and noise so people shout out their answers and move quickly to stand in like-minded groups.

Step 2: Once groups have formed, walk around and ask each group their answer to your question. If it's their favourite sports to play, answers might include tennis, soccer, football and so on. Be encouraging and point out how diverse the groups are.

Step 3: Repeat this exercise at least four times. Have a watch handy and time the group as they hunt for 'human treasures' who are like them, encouraging the group to get faster with each round.

The challenge here is to pick fun and quirky topics that will divide your attendees into many different groups, such as: favourite takeaway food, most used smartphone app or preferred shoe colour. Avoid political, religious or personal characteristics. This exercise is not supposed to make people feel uncomfortable. It's a way to celebrate their similarities and their differences. People who stand together for one topic are usually in a completely different group the next time.

As a wrap-up, explain that everyone brings with them unique and diverse experiences and preferences that you want to tap into and harness throughout the ideation workshop.

4. Top Ten Idea Killers

Every business has them. Those instant idea-killing phrases that get trotted out whenever someone suggests an idea that the business doesn't want to pursue. A simple way to ensure an idea-generation workshop generates a feeling of trust, and permission to take risks with new ideas, is to capture these ingrained idea-killing phrases and ban them from your ideation workshop.

Here's how you do it:

TOP 10 IDEA KILLERS

Step 1: Ask people to name the top ten idea-killing phrases that regularly come up in their business. The usual suspects include: 'That will cost too much,' 'We don't have the time or money,' and 'Our boss won't like that.' People usually have fun citing these phrases, as they've heard them so often and been on the receiving end of them.

Step 2: Write these ten phrases on a flipchart and explain to the group that, just for today, you're banning these phrases.

Step 3: Ask for group agreement that if anyone uses these idea-killing phrases throughout the day, they will buy everyone a drink in the next break time.

This contract is a fun way to deter any naysayers from voicing their doubts and ingrained idea-killing phrases during the ideation workshop.

Remember, these four energisers shouldn't all be done at once. Spread them throughout your ideation workshop to keep encouraging the behaviours you want people to adopt, rather than allowing them to lapse back into a 'business as usual' mindset.

FOUR MUST-HAVES FOR IDEATION SUCCESS

To get the most out of every ideation workshop, there are four more tips I'd like to share with you. These tips will ensure you are fully prepared, get the most out of your workshop attendees and stay on track throughout your session.

1. Location, Location, Location

It's distracting and disruptive to have attendees ducking in and out of an ideation workshop. The best way to prevent this is to set the location of your idea-generating session away from your usual business premises. I know it's tempting to go low cost and use your own meeting room. Trust me, it's worth breaking out. An offsite location sets clear expectations that attendees will stay for the whole time. Otherwise, I find that people act like they're on a bus, hopping on or off whenever another business priority pops up and lures them away.

Working off-site also encourages a siege-like mentality – you're all in it together and no one leaves until the job is done. The other benefit is that you can pick an inspiring space that has loads of natural light, an outdoor break area, great food options, and easy parking or transport links. Then the ideation workshop feels like a reward for attendees rather than hard work.

2. Pre-work

I like to set a pre-work task for everyone who attends an ideation workshop, which is easy and fun to do. It warms people up to your innovation challenge before they arrive and provides more stimuli to help generate ideas, such as pictures, product samples, videos or music. Give people sufficient time to do their pre-work by setting it at least one week in advance. It could be a request like: 'Please bring three beverages that you've never tried before that are healthy and refreshing,' or 'Please bring three snacks that you offer friends when they come over.' Whatever the pre-work task, it should clearly link back to your innovation challenge.

3. Flow of the Day

The most frequent question I get asked is how long an ideation workshop should be and what the right agenda flow is. I usually recommend setting aside one day per innovation challenge, as this allows you to generate new product ideas for three to four Opportunity Springboards.

Here's what the flow of an ideation workshop I would run looks like:

Ideation Workshop Flow

Welcome & objectives of the day.
Energiser: Say My Name & Yes But, Yes And...

1st Creative round
Groups ideate on an Opportunity Springboard
Show and share ideas

— — — — — — — — MORNING BREAK — — — — — — — —

Energiser: Top 10 Idea Killers

2nd & 3rd Creative round
Groups ideate on an Opportunity Springboard
Show and share ideas

— — — — — — — — LUNCH BREAK — — — — — — — —

Energiser: Treasure Hunt

4th Creative round
Groups ideate on an Opportunity Springboard
Show and share ideas

— — — — — — — — AFTERNOON BREAK — — — — — — — —

Love Vote

4. Love Vote

'Lisa, is that a Product Idea page in your pocket?'

'Um... yes. It's just that I noticed my idea for Christmas Nut Snacks didn't get selected and I really would like to make that one happen, so I thought I'd just take it with me...'

I've come to recognise that guilty, glittery-eyed look of someone smuggling a new product idea out of an ideation workshop. I love it when this happens. It means people are so passionate about their idea that they refuse to let it go. I have personally been guilty of shouting excitedly, 'That one! Make that one! It's brilliant!' in more than one ideation workshop.

Now is the time for you to harness the power of emotion. Innovation projects fall over all the time in businesses. Because as soon as they become too expensive, hard to make or hit a delay, the project leader often kills the project. Unless they are emotionally and passionately involved, that is. Then they fight tooth and nail to overcome hurdles and push it forward.

You need people who are so hooked on their new product ideas that they refuse to give up on them, no matter what adversity they face. People like Carolyn Creswell, founder of Carman's, one of Australia's leading muesli businesses. At eighteen years old, Carolyn was at risk of losing her part-time job when the handmade muesli business she worked for was closing down. Instead, Carolyn offered to buy their muesli recipe for $1,000 and continued building the business as a part-time university student. Carman's now sells market-leading muesli-based cereals and snacks worldwide, and is a multi-million dollar business. Now that's the power of passion.

The very last activity of your ideation workshop is to sort and select the top ideas with your exhausted and exhilarated innovation team. As these are the people who created them, it makes sense to understand which product ideas excite your team the most. You're going to do a Love Vote. This is by no means the only idea-sorting criteria you will use. However, it's a fast way to get a sense of what your team would personally love to work on while the ideas are hot and fresh in everyone's minds.

Here's how you do it:

> **Step 1:** Give everyone three green sticky dots.
>
> **Step 2:** Stick up on the wall all the Product Idea pages that you've written.
>
> **Step 3:** Ask everyone to review all the Product Idea pages and put one green dot on the three ideas they love the most. Not what they think the business should make, launch or sell. What they *personally* would want to work on because it excites and inspires them so much.
>
> **Step 4:** Tally up how many votes each new product idea got.
>
> **Step 5:** Pull out those ideas that got one, two or three-plus votes.

How many green-dotted product ideas do you have? The aim is to get to a shortlist of about twenty ideas. Make sure you include any ideas that personally caught your eye. As project owner, it's your prerogative to have a few extra favourites thrown in the mix.

Don't throw away all the ideas that didn't get selected at this stage. Scan in each Product Idea page and save it in a file labelled 'Ideas Bank'. Just like a savings account, you will go back to these ideas when you need them.

Key Learnings and Actions

Now that you've created heaps of original new ideas, you're ready to move on to Stage 4, where you will co-create and road test your top product ideas with the real boss of your innovation challenge – your consumers. But first, here's a summary of the key learnings and actions from Stage 3.

KEY LEARNINGS

- Idea-nurturing behaviour is essential for supporting new and incomplete ideas so that they can mature into more robust, commercially feasible ideas later on.

- Critical thinking is lateral, precise and intolerant of ambiguity. It is best suited to 'business as usual' tasks.

- Creative thinking is expansive, curious and makes new connections. It is vital for successful idea generation.

- Creativity hacks can help move you and your team up the Idea Creativity Spectrum so you can generate more original new product ideas.

- A Product Idea page helps convert open-ended thoughts into specific ideas that you can do something with.

- The aim of an ideation workshop is to generate a high quantity of original ideas. These sessions work better at an offsite meeting location, with clear roles and creative energisers to encourage diversity, equality and idea-nurturing behaviour.

KEY ACTIONS

- Go to: **www.eatdrinkinnovate.com.au/if-bonus** and download the free Product Idea template to complete your Stage 3 Accelerate tasks.

- Set a date and find an offsite venue for your ideation workshop.

- Set a pre-work task to get people thinking about your innovation challenge in advance and bring in stimuli as inspiration.

- Recruit a facilitator and run an amazing ideation workshop by doing the four creative hacks outlined in this stage to generate fresh and original ideas.

- Turn your thoughts into ideas on Product Idea pages and capture more than eighty to one hundred new product ideas.

- Use a Love Vote to select the best twenty ideas to take forward.

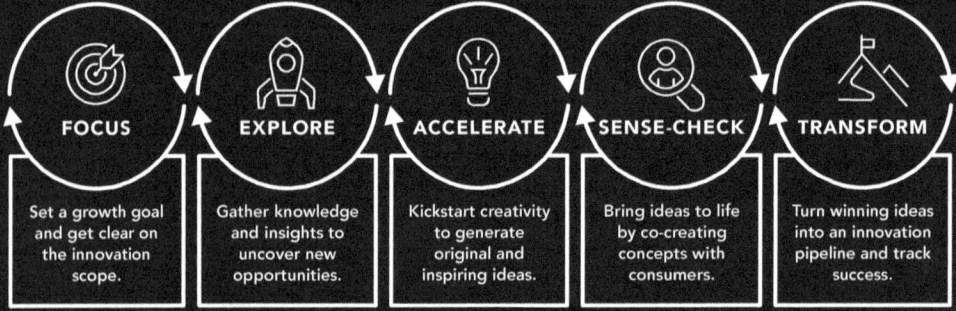

FOCUS

Set a growth goal and get clear on the innovation scope.

EXPLORE

Gather knowledge and insights to uncover new opportunities.

ACCELERATE

Kickstart creativity to generate original and inspiring ideas.

SENSE-CHECK

Bring ideas to life by co-creating concepts with consumers.

TRANSFORM

Turn winning ideas into an innovation pipeline and track success.

you are here

STAGE 4:

Sense-Check

'If you're not prepared to be wrong,
you'll never come up with anything original.'
– *Ken Robinson*

You have come away from your ideation workshop on a high. It was great fun, high energy, and generated lots of inspiring and original product ideas. That's the heady stuff of innovation.

Now, a word of caution. The first thing that usually happens after an ideation workshop is that other people in your business ask how it went and press you to share some of the ideas you came up with.

Here's how that conversation might play out:

Co-worker: How did the ideation workshop on Friday go? What's the best idea you had?

You: Well, the one I love the most features those foil-lined resealable packs. No one has used them with our products before and it would make them really easy to snack on.

Co-worker: What? We don't have a supplier for those. I think they're made overseas, so we could get slammed on the import costs. Then there's the amount of product breakage you'd get in transit. Hmm, we'd have to do a lot of trials, and probably add a whole new outer carton. That's going to be really hard and expensive to do...

Do *not* naively share your newborn ideas with anyone outside of your innovation team, because they're simply not ready for it yet. From the moment you walk out of your ideation workshop, have your core team and anyone else involved in the session go dark. By that, I mean this is the time to go beneath the 'business as usual' radar. You need to become like a silent ninja force that doesn't reveal its secrets. Why? Because once you've stepped out of your idea-nurturing session and back into the cold, hard light of the commercial business, this is the second most common time for new ideas to die prematurely. One stray idea revealed by the photocopier and business reality rains on your parade. Outside of the nurturing hothouse of idea-generation, the business is ready and waiting with its critical thinking, demanding perfect and complete ideas. You don't have them yet.

This next stage is all about building and strengthening your new product ideas, and letting go of the weak non-starters. Until you've done that, here's what you should say to curious co-workers:

> **Co-worker:** How did the ideation workshop on Friday go? What's the best idea you had?

> **You**: It was terrific – we got heaps of amazing new ideas. We're evaluating them now and will share a recommendation on which to progress with once we've thoroughly sense-checked them.

Do not agree to share early ideas with senior management at this stage. Do not tell your friend in accounting. Do not ask other people which ones they like the best. From now on, you only share product ideas on a need-to-know basis, when that person can help you sense-check and select the right ideas to proceed with.

And how do you do that exactly? This section will outline how to narrow down your list of ideas using the ICE model, how to turn your remaining ideas into compelling product concepts, how to co-create ideas with your consumer, and how to know whether you should kill or keep your new product ideas.

Put Your Ideas on ICE

I was speaking at an industry event to fruit and vegetable growers who wanted to turn their raw produce into value-added products. After my presentation on how to create original new product ideas, a mushroom grower approached me.

'I've already got heaps of product ideas,' he said. 'My grocery buyer says he'll range any product I make, because he's so interested in fresh, natural mushroom products.'

'That sounds great,' I replied. 'So, what have you gone ahead with?'

'Nothing,' he muttered gloomily. 'For the past six months, I've been debating with my team. We don't know how to choose the right ones to make.'

'Okay, you need to know the secret to choosing which ideas to go forward with. It's as simple as ICE,' I replied.

Before I reveal to you what ICE stands for, and how it can help you sense-check your ideas, let's do a quick recap.

You should now be holding about twenty roughly written Product Idea pages that your innovation team helped select. It's time to sort the good from the bad and the ugly. This is where a lot of businesses get bogged down and end up going around in circles. They're not sure how to sort through so many new product ideas and find the diamonds in the rough. It's also when innovation agencies ask for their fee and leave, because they've delivered an agreed number of ideas. Whether any of those product ideas are worth progressing further is your problem.

The reason people get confused, overwhelmed and anxious at this stage is they're not sure what criteria to apply to idea selection. It's confusing because it's multi-dimensional. Many of the new ideas you now have may be uninspiring or impractical. You need to turn them into desirable, feasible and viable ideas. This is challenging for a number of reasons. First, it's likely your business has existing manufacturing capabilities that it would prefer to leverage instead of investing in new ones. Second, you probably operate in a crowded marketplace, with savvy competitors constantly innovating and watching your every move. And third, your consumers aren't really good at projecting into the future and telling you what products they want.

To overcome these challenges, you need to find those new product ideas that sit within the Innovation Sweet Spot.

What do I mean by the Innovation Sweet Spot? I've found that the best new product opportunities meet three key requirements:

1. **Consumer**: It satisfies a consumer want, need or wish.

2. **Capability**: You can source, produce and sell it.

3. **Category**: There is a commercial gain to be made in the marketplace.

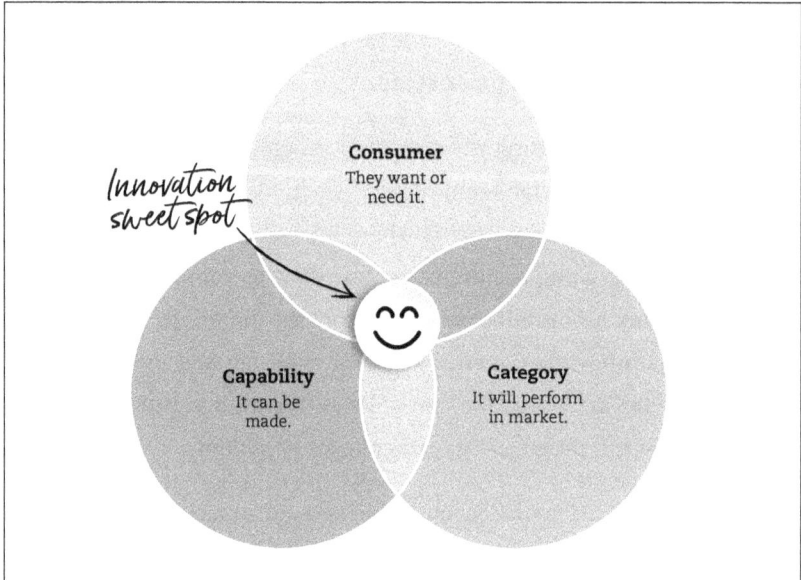

If your new product idea meets all three of these requirements, you've hit the Innovation Sweet Spot. For example, imagine I'm a milk producer looking to create other new dairy products because my milk is becoming commoditised due to price decreases by retailers. I already have milk-processing equipment, and so I've generated a lot of new ideas that I could make with my existing operational capabilities, with some modifications, such as cheese, yoghurt, butter and ice cream. Reviewing these, one of my ideas is unique and breakthrough for the category – a cholesterol-lowering cheese. I test this idea with consumers and discover that they are really interested in healthier cheeses. This new product idea falls within the Innovation Sweet Spot. Meaning, I can make it, it will have a significant category impact (being new and unique), and consumers want it.

By considering these three areas as screening and selection criteria, you ensure that your new product ideas will be:

- **Desirable:** People will really want to buy them. Remember the secret to new product success? Find out what consumers want first, then find a way to make it. This ensures a 'pull' strategy in-market, whereby demand for your product is so strong it's literally pulled off the shelves by your consumers, not 'pushed' onto them by you.

- **Feasible:** You'll be able to make them in the short or long term. As a business that has some products in the market, chances are you already have some manufacturing, product development and selling capability. You'd be crazy to walk away from all that investment and skill without first seeing if there's any way you could repurpose it to deliver a new product (with some modifications, additions or upgrades). The important thing to remember, though, is not to start with this goal in mind. Consumer need first, capability second. You may also have to be open-minded to the possibility that for a big enough idea – that consumers truly love, which would reignite a category – you may need to invest in new equipment, or partner with external suppliers, to bring new capabilities into your business.

- **Viable:** There is a commercial opportunity in the marketplace. This is your sustainable growth check to make sure that your new product – which consumers love, and which you can make – actually stands a fighting chance of lasting for more than six months when pit against the existing competitive set in the market. To do this, your new product needs to be fairly unique, different and able to provide sales growth by improving a current product for current users, attracting new users or creating a new market.

Sense-checking your new product ideas against the three Innovation Sweet Spot criteria will help you decide which ones to pursue. How do you do it? This is where the ICE model comes in.

The ICE model was developed by tech entrepreneur Sean Ellis to help rank growth ideas. ICE stands for Impact, Confidence and Ease, and each criteria question relates to a different Innovation Sweet Spot requirement:

1. **What is the Category Impact?** If this idea works, how big an impact will it have? How much will it grow your business and the marketplace?

2. **What is the Consumer Confidence?** How much do your consumers want it?

3. **What is the Capability Ease?** How easy would it be to make this product?

Idea Sense-Checking

How *confident* are you that consumers want it?

Consumer
They want or need it.

How *easy* is it to make and launch?

Capability
It can be made.

Category
It will perform in market.

How big an *impact* will it have in market?

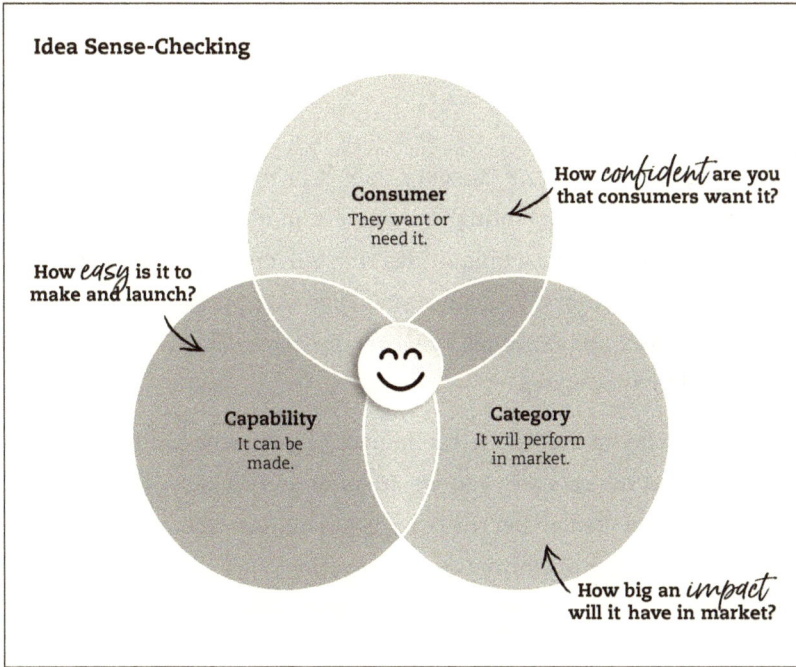

Here's how you use it:

Step 1: Gather your innovation project team. Together, give each new product idea an ICE score for each of the three criteria, ranging from one to ten. A score of ten is for something that's really amazing, while a score of one is for something that's no good at all. This is where it really helps to have some functional expertise to assist with this ranking. These people may already be on your innovation team. If not, invite some subject matter experts in to help you do this. They need to know about supply chain operations, the competitive market environment and your desired consumers.

Step 2: If a new product idea gets a score of ten for impact, ten for confidence and ten for ease, it's a brilliant idea that you should progress. An idea scoring one for impact, confidence and ease should be killed off straightaway before it wastes any more valuable time and resource.

So, how do you get these scores? Let's dive into the way you should sense-check each Innovation Sweet Spot attribute.

CATEGORY IMPACT

I like to start by assessing Category Impact because it's very tangible – most businesses are operating in a current marketplace with existing competitors. If you have a unique idea that will create a whole new, never-seen-before category, you can simply give that product idea a ten for Category Impact and move on. However, for the majority of your ideas, you'll need to do this step.

The easiest way to determine the impact of your new product ideas is to understand the category you would enter and consider what already exists in market. Remember the three types of innovation from Stage 1 – core, adjacent and transformational innovation? Now is the time to bring this knowledge back in, to determine which type of innovation your product ideas fall under. This will help you determine the commercial impact they could have in the category they will play in.

I like using the Innovation Spectrum Model, developed by Happen innovators.

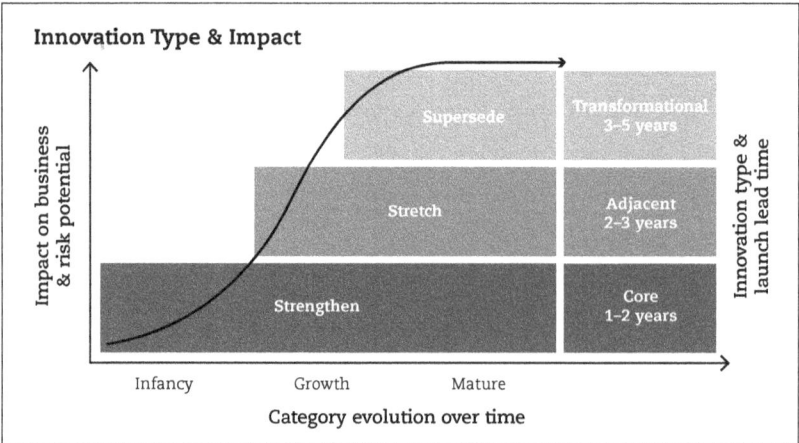

Source: Full Spectrum of Innovation, Happen, 2015

It shows the different impact each type of innovation can have, depending on the category lifecycle your new product ideas will be playing in:

- **Strengthen:** Core innovation (usually created over one to two years) builds and strengthens your existing products through incremental changes, like new flavour extensions, new ingredient additions and design improvements. It's continuous, with relatively low cost and low impact. This is like adding an organic coconut flavour to an existing range of Greek yoghurts. This type of innovation works well in categories which are in their infancy and still growing, as it attracts new users and increases the purchase repertoire of existing users. If you have ideas like this, give them a Low Impact score (between one and four).

- **Stretch:** Adjacent innovation (usually created over two to three years) drives extra growth through bigger product changes – such as new recipes, product formats or packaging – which stretch into categories that are new to your business and adjacent to your existing products. It tends to generate more impact and sales return because it opens up new market or consumer opportunities. This would be like adding a new range of low-sugar, Greek yoghurts in squeezy tubes for young kids to your existing yoghurt products. This type of innovation works well in growing markets that are becoming crowded with competitors, as it helps you attract new sets of consumers, while still leveraging your brand or product capability. If you have new product ideas like this, give them a Medium Impact score (between five and seven).

- **Supersede:** Transformational innovation (done over three to five years) can be high risk but potentially high impact as it supersedes existing categories or products. These are usually new-to-market products that create a whole new category that didn't previously exist, satisfying a new consumer group. For example, in the US, Chobani *superseded* grocery-bought yoghurts with the launch of a Chobani Café, which serves Greek yoghurt made from hand-selected artisanal ingredients. If you have new product ideas that access a new market or consumers, give them a High Impact score (between eight and ten).

If you want your new product ideas to succeed, you need to understand your category lifecycle stage and ensure you're bringing to market the right type of innovation to make the impact you need.

Here's how you get your Category Impact Score:

Step 1: Go back to your new product ideas. What product category would these play in? Assign each category a lifecycle stage – infancy, growth or mature. If you're not sure, consider the existing products in the category and the type of new products being launched there. This will give you a good insight into the category lifecycle stage.

Step 2: Look at your new product ideas. What type of innovation are they in relation to your existing business and products – core, adjacent or transformational?

Step 3: For each new product idea, considering its innovation type and the category it will play in, what impact will it likely have in the marketplace?

Would it be:

- Core – Strengthen strategy (Low Impact; score of one to four).
- Adjacent – Stretch strategy (Medium Impact; score of five to seven).
- Transformational – Supersede strategy (High Impact; score of eight to ten).

Step 4: Give each of your new product ideas a broad development timeframe. You'll get a better handle on this once you do the Capability Ease review. However, you may already be able to say (based on the type of innovation it is) whether a product idea would take up to one year, two to three years, or three to five years to develop and launch.

This is a great sense-check exercise to make sure you haven't given in to the temptation to choose only one type of innovation over another. Ultimately, you're looking for a healthy mix of some easy, close-in product ideas, which you can launch quickly with low risk and minimal investment, and some transformational ideas, which are riskier but could have massive returns.

Remember the seventy-twenty-ten rule from Stage 1? How close to the Golden Ratio is your mix of new product ideas? By default, most businesses choose core innovation ideas. That's a great way to leverage existing assets. However, just remember to keep in at least ten per cent of those hair-raising, terrifying, transformational new product ideas too. After the three to five years it may take to make them, they might be exactly what your business needs to kickstart growth.

If your final mix of product ideas is too heavily swayed in either direction, revisit some of those ideas in your Ideas Bank (which we spoke about at the end of Stage 3). Check whether there are any gems you could resurrect or redevelop to help balance out your innovation mix. Also consider whether you could change some of your existing ideas. Push them harder into more stretching options, or tame them so they're more familiar and close-in.

CAPABILITY EASE

We're going to jump to the 'E' in ICE now – Capability Ease – because it's important to determine your capabilities with regard to your product ideas. If you have a supply chain or product development team member who has been itching to ground your ideas in reality, they will love this stage. This is when you do a top-line review of which new product ideas your business will be able to make in the next one to five years.

This is the time to consider your current capabilities in manufacturing, supply, sourcing and distribution, as well as talking with new potential external suppliers. Your goal is to understand the complexity, cost and time required to bring your new product ideas to market.

A couple of key areas I like to evaluate at this stage include:

- Packaging complexity.
- Production complexity.
- Raw ingredient availability.
- Capital expenditure required.
- Supplier availability.
- Development lead time.

Consider this a starting list – feel free to add to it with your supply team.

I've seen some amazing spreadsheets rating and weighting each of these factors separately, and then tallying them up to reach an overall Capability Ease score. At this stage, that is overkill. Keep it simple by thinking about *your own business's* current capability for each product idea and what you could do using *other external* suppliers, contractors or businesses. Then evaluate each new product idea and assign a Capability Ease score by answering the following questions:

- **Is this product similar to others in your business?** If you could make this new product straightaway with some simple, low-cost changes, give the idea a High Ease score (nine to ten).

- **Is this product new to your business?** If other businesses in the same category are currently offering this product, then the capability exists for this product type, so give the idea a Medium Ease score (between six and eight).

- **Is this product new to the category?** If other product categories are making this type of product, then the capability exists, just not for your category yet, so give the idea a Lower Ease score (between three and five).

- **Is this product new to the world?** If no one is making this product yet, and it has yet to be invented, the good news is that you've come up with a world first! The bad news is you're going to have to invest significant time and money to create your product from scratch. Give the idea a Lowest Ease score (between one and two).

At this stage, there is a tendency for people to cut out all the hard, transformational ideas and keep all the small, easy-to-make ones. However, remember that you're looking for a healthy balance of core, adjacent and transformational ideas to maximise business growth. Conversely, if all your product ideas have Low Ease scores, this is a risky strategy, as you may have to spend a lot of resources developing this capability. If this is the case, try scaling back some of your new product ideas so that they're easier to make in the short to medium term.

At this stage, it's too soon to cut out any new product ideas entirely, even those with Low Ease scores, as you're still missing the key piece to the idea-selection puzzle. That is, understanding what your consumers want.

CONSUMER CONFIDENCE

Now it's time to consider your consumers. This is the stage that a lot of businesses get wrong because they launch straight into full-scale product development, without confirming product-market fit first.

Stop right now.

This step is going to save you lots of heartache, time and money. I've deliberately left the Consumer Confidence score until last because it's the deal-breaker. Consumers are your ultimate boss.

At this stage, you need to understand consumers' reactions to your product ideas. If they want changes made to your new product ideas, this will also change the Capability Ease and Category Impact of each idea.

Before we get into how to get your Consumer Confidence score, there are three key metrics you need to know about which help indicate whether a consumer wants or needs a new product idea or not. I found these to be the most predictive of in-market product success. I call these the Consumer Confidence Trifecta: likeability, uniqueness and purchase intent.

I'll explain why these are important first. Then, in the next section, we'll explore how you can measure these yourselves to attain a Consumer Confidence score for your new product ideas.

1. Likeability: How much do people like your product idea?

There has to be a degree of emotional liking from consumers for your new product. It needs to appeal to them. Not many people buy food or drinks based purely on a functional need any more – there's usually an emotional component to our choices, based on our underlying needs or wants. Let's take bottled water, for example. It's a very basic product that should be a straightforward choice. However, if I were buying a bottle of water purely because I was thirsty, then I would buy the closest and cheapest bottle of water I could find, without much thought. However, the majority of people pause at the drinks fridge and consider the staggering range available. This is when subtle emotional drivers kick in. Do you want to ensure your money is put towards worthy causes? Then you might pick up a bottle of Thankyou water, which donates all profits to charity. Or if you believe in the quality of water from a clean spring source, then you might choose Evian. Since a lot of food and beverage products need to appeal on an emotional level as well as a functional one, your consumer must find your new product ideas desirable. Likeability is a simple way to measure this. I'll show you how to measure it with two simple tools in the next section.

I believe likeability is the most important of the three metrics. After all, you need your product to be likeable so consumers want to try it. If they dislike it on sight, the other two metrics are irrelevant because consumers will never even pick it up to consider it.

2. Uniqueness: How different is your product idea?

To survive in today's crowded marketplace, your new product must be unique and differentiated in some way to warrant consumers' attention. Uniqueness doesn't mean you must have a totally original new product. Uniqueness can come from a range of different sources, including branding, packaging, method of use, graphic design, flavours, ingredients or source of origin, to name a few.

Consider again the world of bottled water. How on earth can a new product in that category be different or unique? After all, it's all just clear water in a bottle. Or is it? These water products go to great lengths to differentiate themselves on provenance (where the water is from), quality (its clean/pure/natural credentials), packaging (bottle shape/size/material), benefits (escapism, purity, thirst-quenching, image-building, social benefit), and positioning (high-end boutique/reassuringly mainstream/good value).

Uniqueness is important because, if you want your product to succeed in the long term, it needs to be perceived as being different from what's already on offer in the market so that it stands out. 'Me-too' products, which differentiate themselves only on price, usually lead short lives because they don't have any truly unique features.

3. Purchase intent: Would people buy your new product idea instead of, or in addition to, existing products?

No matter how likeable and unique your new product ideas are, you need to know whether consumers would part with their hard-earned cash to buy it. The challenge here is that people usually only buy a certain amount of each product type. This is called their purchase repertoire.

Your challenge is whether your new product will be valued enough to encourage consumers to replace, or add to, what they're already buying.

For example, consider your fridge at home. How many different types of milk do you have in there? Mine has three types: low-fat dairy milk for my children, coconut milk for my health-conscious husband and unsweetened almond milk for my coffee. So, my milk-buying repertoire is three products. If I'm having friends over, however, and I know one of them is lactose-intolerant, I buy soy milk and add this to my existing purchases, so my buying repertoire increases to four products. The key here is that your new product must offer either better or incremental benefits, which are worth buying.

Sometimes consumers want to please you when you ask them about their purchase intentions and will, therefore, say they'll 'try anything once'. The key is to really challenge this default statement. Would they really try it? Would they *not* pick up their favourite product and instead put your new product in their shopping basket instead?

Here's an example of how I measured a new product idea across all three Consumer Confidence metrics to get a sense of how strong my new product ideas were. I was sense-checking eleven new tea blends among dedicated tea-drinkers to work out which ideas to proceed with. It was a tough market to crack, as these tea-lovers already bought between seven and ten different tea products. They were already really satisfied with their existing buying repertoire, and I was exploring whether there was room for a new tea product.

Of the ideas I tested with these consumers, here were the findings:

- Three tea blends were wildly unique but for all the wrong reasons. Yes, they were completely new blends that hadn't been combined before. Unfortunately, consumers really didn't like the blends and wouldn't even be tempted to try them.

- Three ideas were well liked because they were very similar to competitor products. However, they weren't unique enough to be bought instead of these existing options. These ideas needed an extra point of difference and unique benefit to encourage trial and purchase.

- Five ideas were well liked and sufficiently unique to encourage trial ahead of existing competitor products. These were a winning combination of new tea blends, in new packaging, with new-to-market health benefits.

Can you see how a combination of the three Consumer Confidence metrics can help you decide which new product ideas to proceed with? It also helps you understand which ideas need improving or culling.

Before we move on, a quick word of warning. When sense-checking product ideas with consumers, don't be tempted to ask consumers about the relevance of a product idea. It sounds like a good thing to check, but consumers tend to overthink and over-rationalise this measure. They may give you the most logical answer about a product idea, rather than what they really feel. For example, I've had consumers rate a new chocolate bar as low relevance, but high on intended purchase. This means that while they might not need it, they sure want to buy it. Measures like relevance work better for functional products like dishwashing detergent or stain removers, not emotionally fuelled food and beverage products.

Now you know what consumer metrics are the most important to understand the potential of a new product idea. In the next section I'm going to show you how to share your ideas in a way that allows you to co-create and optimise them directly with your consumers. This will provide you with those essential Consumer Confidence scores and confirm which ideas to progress, and which to cut out early.

Create a Compelling Product Concept

To share ideas with consumers, you need to create a prototype. A prototype is a basic, tangible representation of your product idea that makes it testable. You're looking for the simplest, cheapest and most basic way you can show your product idea to consumers, so that you can learn and fail as early and cheaply as possible. No one likes to fail – but it's a crucial part of the learning process. My kids' school has a great acronym for the word fail: First attempt in learning. Let's adopt that mindset.

The principle behind prototype testing is to discover the weaknesses and strengths of your product idea quickly. That way, you can improve it or lose it before you've spent heaps of time, effort and resources on it. The longer you wait to test an idea or product, the more you've invested in it, which means it becomes more expensive to fail.

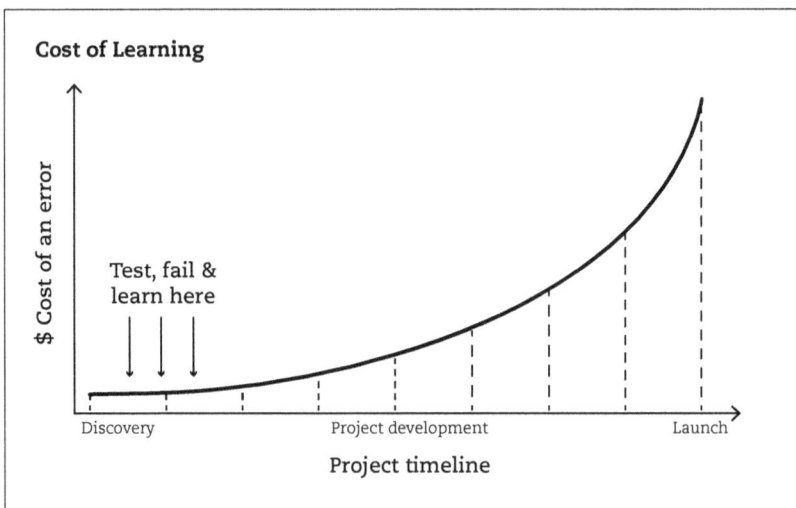

It's best to test your new product ideas with consumers at every stage throughout the product development process. In the front-end discovery stage, you start with a prototype – as the simplest, cheapest and easiest option. Once you're confident an idea is worth pursuing, then you go on to test more tangible product representations – like a bench-made sample or final product and packaging.

I use a product concept as a prototype at this stage. A product concept is simply a written and visual expression of your idea for consumers to react to. It's so much easier to rub out a word, or redraw a picture if you've got an idea horribly wrong, then remake a finished product from scratch.

While consumers can't tell you what to make, they are brilliant at responding to product ideas. It's important that your ideas have enough substance and detail for consumers to react to at this early stage. With their feedback, you can refine and strengthen your product ideas.

The good news is that you can create product concepts to share with consumers by yourself. Here's an example of what a product concept looks like, from one of my nut snacking ideas in Stage 3:

Product Concept

Kale Nut Smoothie

Introducing our new Kale Nut Smoothie, for a naturally nutritious, on-the-go breakfast.

This deliciously creamy smoothie packs a nutritional punch. It contains finely blended kale, apple and almond milk, making it low in calories and high in iron, fibre, vitamin A and antioxidants.

It's perfect for when you want to start the day with a natural boost, and don't have time to prepare breakfast.

Image source: To & Fro (lifestyle blog), 2017

A product concept needs to have four key features:

1. **A name:** This explains what the product is. Don't get too tricky with names here – simple, clear language is best, as consumers are more likely to understand it. I also avoid brand names, because I want a clean read on how strong the ideas are without any known branding. In the example above, the name of the product is Kale Nut Smoothie. It doesn't get much simpler than that.

2. **A product description:** This explains what the product is, giving as many familiar references as possible to suggest the product experience, such as its taste, texture, size, and expectations of flavour and smell. In my example, the product description states: 'This deliciously creamy smoothie packs a nutritional punch.' Can you see how a consumer is being invited to imagine the smoothie's taste and texture?

3. **A reason-to-believe:** This describes how the product offers the benefits it does. This can include reasons like the way it's made, its ingredients, its packaging or its usage instructions. In my example, the reason-to-believe is: 'It contains finely blended kale, apple and almond milk, making it low in calories and high in iron, fibre, vitamins A, C and K, and antioxidants.'

4. **A product benefit:** This describes what's in it for the consumer. It highlights what makes it unique, appealing or suitable for them. In my example, the product benefit is: 'It's perfect for when you want to start the day with a natural boost, and don't have time to prepare breakfast.' This suggests the smoothie is easy and quick to prepare, yet still nutritious and filling.

Here are my six top tips to help you create your own compelling product concepts.

1. WRITE LIKE A REAL PERSON

To write winning new product concepts, you've got to cut out industry jargon and use language that a real person would use. This may seem like a no-brainer, but just think of all the acronyms, industry expressions and category jargon you use every day, without even being aware of it. When these are used in product concepts, they confuse and irritate the very people you're trying to attract, because you make it hard for them to understand what you're offering.

My top tips here are to:

- Steer clear of category classifications and describe the product instead. For example, if the product is cheese sticks, refer to it as such – rather than using business expressions like 'ambient dairy'.

- Avoid describing your target consumer using their demographic or sociographic profile, as this can end up sounding like a stereotype. Instead, describe them according to their needs or desires. For example, rather than 'pre-teen snackers, aged nine to eleven years', use simple, more emotive language like: 'For hungry kids wanting to fill up between meals'.

- Avoid using industry packaging or size descriptors. For example, if you're launching new 'product variants' to an existing range, simply introduce them as 'a range of delicious new flavours'.

If in doubt, try reading your concept aloud. Is it how a regular person would speak? Try reading it to someone outside your business too. Does anything sound weird or jarring? If so, replace the offending words with everyday language.

2. STEER CLEAR OF INSIGHT STATEMENTS

Traditional research or innovation agencies will tell you to always include an 'insight statement' as the first sentence of a new product concept. This is a summary of a consumer's need, want or problem. For example, 'I find it hard to get grass stains out of my white clothes.'

This approach was designed to stop product innovators from offering unwanted stuff to consumers. Unfortunately, what usually happens is that these 'insights' are written so badly that people are turned off your idea in the very first sentence. If the product concept were for a new chocolate bar, for example, would you really agree with the insight 'I want to add more joy to my life'? That's a real example, by the way, and I can tell you it didn't go down well with consumers.

Don't get me wrong. Your product ideas must satisfy a user need, want or problem to have any chance of sustainable success in-market. However, if you've completed Stage 2 and created new product ideas from your Opportunity Springboards, then your ideas will already be grounded in consumer insights. Remember in my Opportunity Springboard example 'Veggie Snack Attack', the 'why' section ensured that we focused on helping teenagers who wanted to eat more vegetables but found it a hassle to peel, cut and prepare them. If you think you've gone off track with some of your new product ideas, go back and check whether they satisfy your original Opportunity Springboards. If so, you're in the clear. It's safer not to irritate consumers by including an insight that tells them what they should think or feel.

3. THE MORE YOU SAY, THE MORE YOU'LL LEARN

When writing the product description of your product concept, the biggest challenge is not including enough detail for your consumer to give actionable feedback. Broad and generic-sounding product ideas usually cause confusion, low likeability and less desire to buy. It also means you don't learn which specific elements of your new idea are good or bad.

For example, if I offered you a slice of bread, how do you know whether you'd like it and want to buy it? Given the numerous types of bread available, chances are you'd struggle to give me meaningful feedback about this idea. Now, what if I offered you a thickly cut slice of handmade sourdough bread, with a chewy texture and crisp crust? You could tell me what elements you do and don't like, so I can change and improve the idea based on your needs and wants. If you didn't like the idea of chewy bread, I could make it soft. Or if you didn't like the thick-cut size, I could make it finely sliced.

It's critical to include specific details about the expected flavour, texture, shape or size of your new product. For example, will it be spicy, zesty, crunchy, smooth, thin, thick, bite-size? This also helps when it comes to actual product development, because you can direct your team to create the desired look, feel and taste your consumers want and expect.

4. USE MAGIC WORDS FOR PRODUCT BENEFITS

When expressing the product benefit in your concept, it helps to find and use your category's 'magic words' to boost consumer appeal. Every category has these – they represent a must-have benefit regardless of the product type, flavour or format.

For example, in the hair-colour category, the magic words include universally sought-after benefits, such as 'vibrant', 'glossy' and 'rich'. These are desired by every hair-colour user, regardless of what shade of hair colour they want. It's the opposite of dull, lifeless, faded colour – the enemy of every hair-colour user.

For food categories, these magic words tend to be appetite-driving words, such as 'delicious', 'enticing' or 'moreish'. For drink categories, it may be benefits like 'refreshing', 'light' or 'sparkling'. Listen to your consumers as they talk about your product idea. Magic words usually pop up when they express their wants and needs.

5. MAKE THE 'REASON TO BELIEVE' COMPELLING

This means explaining how your idea delivers its benefit and why users should believe you. Some reasons to believe are functional, such as:

- The ingredients it does or doesn't contain. For example: 'This product contains a delicious blend of raw walnuts and chia seeds that are rich in protein.' Or: 'With fifty per cent less sugar than other energy drinks.'

- The way it is made. For example: 'Cold-pressed to retain more nutrients.'

- Where it comes from. For example: 'Sourced from the remote wilderness of South West Tasmania.'

- The type of packaging and how it works. For example: 'Available in a handy, resealable bag.'

Other new product ideas have emotional reasons to believe. Don't avoid or apologise for these. Call them out because, to the right consumer, they will be really important and motivating. These may be benefits such as:

- The look or type of packaging. For example: 'In a beautifully embossed, glass bottle.'

- The way it will make you feel. For example: 'You'll feel as healthy on the inside as you do on the outside.'

Just be cautious not to overstate these emotional reasons to believe. No one likes being told their life will be transformed by a pre-mixed salad or loaf of bread – unless it's done with tongue-in-cheek humour. Even then, make sure it's funny and appropriate for your end consumer.

6. SHOW RATHER THAN TELL

Some businesses like to avoid the time and cost of drawing pictures of their new product ideas if they have many to sense-check. I can guarantee that any visualisation of your product idea is better than nothing at all. When testing a product concept, I've seen consumers latch onto a great visual and overcome poorly worded or confusing copy, as product visuals are so much more effective at bringing to life a new idea.

For example, I could tell you about an idea for a self-heating, cardboard egg box. It boils an egg in two minutes without water and is made with chemical layers surrounding the egg that produce heat when activated. Can you even imagine what I'm talking about, based on words alone? Have you pictured something incredibly high-tech and scary looking?

Alternatively, I could show you a picture of it, like the one below. This is the Gogol Mogol, created by the KIAN branding company as a healthy snack. I bet the idea now seems more appealing and easier to use than you imagined from just my written description.

Image source: Gogol Mogol, KIAN, 2017

For the first round of product idea testing, I use a very simple picture of my new products, such as a black-and-white hand sketch, or free stock images from the Internet. It doesn't have to be fancy at this stage – you're simply trying to give people an impression of how the product might look, feel and be used. The easier your picture is to discard, or re-do quickly and cheaply, the better.

For my second or third round of idea testing, I like to increase the visual details as I start getting clearer about what the product should be. Design agencies can create three-dimensional, computer-rendered, colour pictures for you, or you can start bringing in physical samples that represent the right features. Visual and physical prototypes help you solidify what your product idea is really about and test different alternatives of it. Stimuli that helps express the colour, flavour, size, shape, taste, texture or smell will help you learn what consumers want and don't want. For example, you might show consumers a sample bottle of the right dimensions, provide them with fragrance samples or get them to taste key ingredients.

I once used sponges and cotton wool to demonstrate how soft a biscuit centre might be. Consumers could more easily talk through the benefits of one biscuit over another, based on these basic representations, rather than imagining the biscuit centres based only on words on a page.

In the next section, I'm going to tell you how to undertake idea co-creation with consumers, and how to use the three consumer confidence measures (likeability, uniqueness and purchase intent) to identify winning new product ideas to progress further.

Co-Create with Your Consumer

I remember presenting the final packaging for a new body wash to a management team. The general manager, a fifty-five-year-old man, took one look at the bold, floral packaging and said, 'I don't like the look of those flowers – they're too bright and garish. Let's tone them down.'

This is known as general manager (GM) attack. It occurs when a senior manager assumes they share the same needs and preferences as your consumer.

Fortunately, I was prepared. 'Let me just show you what our consumers think,' I suggested and played a video recorded earlier when sharing the pack designs with our desired consumers. It showed real footage of thirteen-to-fifteen-year-old girls raving happily about the striking pack design. Unsurprisingly, the views of teenage girls and our fifty-five-year-old male manager were quite different. The GM gave the go-ahead to proceed.

Now is a critical time to step away from internal opinions and subjective judgements about your new product ideas. You cannot assume that what you or your business colleagues like is the same as what your consumers want. Consumer feedback can help shape lacklustre product ideas into winning ones by redirecting the assumptions, hypotheses or opinions (of you and your business) and enabling you to form truly valued products that people want to buy.

As soon as you have created your new product concepts, it's time to share these with consumers. Concepts can be sense-checked in many ways. At this early stage, I like to use a qualitative interview approach to co-create ideas together. That means talking directly with your consumers to craft and build your ideas with them in real-time. This approach helps you understand what is, or isn't, working with regard to a new product idea and make improvements as you go. I will usually do at least two or three rounds of interviewing with consumers to sense-check my new product ideas. After each round, I rework the product ideas to optimise consumers' liking, uniqueness and purchase intent. It's a fast and effective way to keep evolving your product ideas into stronger, improved offers with very little time, expense and effort.

If you're not confident interviewing people, you can hire someone to do this for you. However, I use an interview approach that is so simple, you will genuinely be able to do this by yourself. Furthermore, if you're self-sufficient when talking with consumers, you'll be able to repeat this stage of sense-checking whenever you need to. Now is a good time to go back to Stage 2 and review the insight-ready behaviour prompts and brush up on your TED interviewing skills.

I suggest you aim to talk with twelve to twenty consumers. This is not meant to be representative of the whole population of potential users. It will, however, give you enough coverage to hear and identify recurring themes in their feedback. Once you start hearing the same responses over and over again, you know you've got enough feedback to make a change to your product concept. Remember, the aim of this exercise is to review, build and craft your new product ideas until they are as strong as they possibly can be.

WHO SHOULD I TALK TO?

If you're in a small business selling directly from your own shop, market stall or website, chances are you're already asking for, and receiving, your consumers' opinions every day. According to research by George Castellion and Stephen K. Markham, because of this consumer closeness, small businesses have lower new product failure rates (ten per cent) than medium to large businesses (forty per cent). It wouldn't take much to build this idea sense-checking approach into your regular selling practices.

If you're working in a medium or large-sized business, there's a high likelihood that you haven't personally spoken with your consumers for a while. That's about to change.

In terms of who you should talk to, if your product ideas are aimed at a specific target market, clearly you should conduct your interviews with that group. For example, concepts for children's breakfast cereals would be tested with parents of young children. However, if you don't have a set target, many grocery products are tested among main or joint household grocery buyers, this typically includes women and men aged between twenty-five to fifty-five plus years old.

I like to talk with current consumers because they can compare and contrast your new product ideas with what they already know in the marketplace. I also like to occasionally use extreme users, as they have some in-depth perspectives about the category. They can also help highlight where your product ideas may be falling short or exceeding expectations.

I sometimes talk with non-product users too, especially if I want to understand how I might entice them into a new or existing category they don't currently buy. Just make sure that the non-users you interview are not 'rejecters'. These are people who would never buy your type of product, no matter how good it is or what you offer. It would simply never be a choice for them, and you're wasting your time and theirs by including them. A simple series of questions can help screen these people out in advance:

Question: Have you ever bought (your idea) type of products?

Answer: No. (This makes them non-users.)

Question: Would you ever consider buying (your idea) type of products?

Answer: Yes. (Great, go ahead and include them in the interview process.)

Answer: No. (This makes them product rejecters. Don't include them in the interview process, as it's a complete waste of time.)

WHAT'S HOT AND WHAT'S NOT

Once you've got a list of people to talk to, it's time to share, build and craft your new product ideas with them. The tool I'm introducing you to is called What's Hot and What's Not. It's an easy way to review your new ideas with consumers, without having to write down or remember a huge list of probing questions in advance. You simply let the template guide you.

In a casual interview setting, with either a small group of consumers or one on one, ask the following six questions and capture your consumers' responses in the What's Hot and What's Not template. I suggest you to film these interviews – a simple smartphone will do the trick. This allows you to play the recording back later, so you can make sense of your scribbled notes. These recordings are also invaluable if you need to justify how or why you took a product idea in a direction that contradicts the views of a senior stakeholder later on. As per my GM-attack experience from earlier on, it reassures people that your decisions are backed by true consumer feedback, not personal preferences, and that's hard to argue with.

What's Hot and What's Not: Idea Feedback

These bits were awesome...	This part needs more work...

I just didn't get it...	What if it could be more...

When you sit down with consumers, show them one new product concept at a time and ask them the following questions:

1. **What do you like about the product idea?** Write their response in the top left-hand quadrant in bullet points. Try to capture direct quotes.

2. **What do you not like about the product idea?** Write their response in the top right-hand quadrant.

3. **Is there anything you don't understand?** Write their response in the bottom left-hand quadrant.

4. **How different is this product idea from what's already available?** Write their response in either the top left-hand quadrant or the top right-hand quadrant, depending on whether it is positive or negative.

5. **Would you buy this product instead of or as well as your usual products? Why or why not?** If the answer is yes, make a note of this in the top left-hand quadrant. If the answer is no, capture this in the top right-hand quadrant. In both instances, make sure you include the reason why.

6. **What could be done to make the product idea better?** Your focus here should be on the benefit, reason to believe, name and picture of the product. Write the consumer's suggestions in the bottom right-hand quadrant.

Take the time after each question to ask additional, TED-style questions (which we discussed in Stage 2) to dive deeper into what they like, dislike, don't understand and want to see improved. Remember, you'll need to be able to action these learnings, so encourage people to be as specific as possible in their answers. Use a different template for each user and collate them all at the end of your interviews for each product concept you shared.

Don't expect the consumers you talk with to rewrite words in your product concept for you. That's taking the idea of co-creation too far. You'll simply waste valuable interviewing time debating the merit of different words. Instead, ask them for suggestions about the meaning or intention they'd like to be expressed, and move on. It's the consumer's job to point you in the right direction. It's your job to pave the way to get there.

NURTURE YOUR IDEAS

After the first round of consumer interviews, people tend to lose faith in their new product ideas, expecting them to excel the first time and killing them off early when they hear a negative response from people.

Here's a reality check. You need to accept the fact that no product idea is ever completely right the first time. This is where it's important to bring back your idea-nurturing behaviour. If you want your product ideas to succeed in the market, you are going to have to invest the time and effort into building those ideas into the strongest versions they can be.

Here's how you do that:

Step 1. Consolidate all your consumer feedback into a single What's Hot and What's Not summary for each new product idea.

Step 2. Look for common feedback themes. What was the strongest message coming through? For example, perhaps the majority of the consumers you interviewed didn't understand the product name, or the flavours were not liked, or the bottle dimensions were wrong. Ignore the odd one-off comments – treat these as anomalies. You're looking for points that most people agreed on.

Here are some prompts to consider:

- Could you simplify the name?
- Was the product description easy to understand?
- Was the product benefit appealing?
- Was the reason-to-believe motivating?
- Were any of the descriptive words sticking points?
- Did the picture bring to life the product and show how it might be used, eaten or stored?

Step 3. Look for clues on how to improve and re-craft your idea. Use consumers' suggestions as inspiration to guide improvements to each product idea. Try to clarify what people didn't understand. Re-move common dislikes. Strengthen and emphasise likes. Use the suggestions provided.

Step 4. Give ideas more than one chance. After one round of interviewing, I always re-work and throw back in even the worst received ideas for a second or third round of feedback. It doesn't hurt to give them another go before you get rid of them.

Sometimes an idea is simply so new that people don't know what to make of it. Don't sanitise or water down these product ideas to overcome this. Instead, try to provide a more familiar frame of reference to help your consumers understand it. For example, the idea of wine in a can is quite foreign to a lot of traditional wine drinkers. However, showing wine in a premium, slimline, aluminium can, which looks and feels like a cider, provides a known frame of reference. It demonstrates how wine could be served in an easy to carry, portable format, which is ideal for people wanting single servings in out-of-home settings like picnics.

REVISIT YOUR IDEAS BANK

This is also a good time to go back to the saved ideas in your Ideas Bank. Remember all those extra ideas you generated back in Stage 3 that you haven't used yet? Go back and mine those now. Are there any product ideas that you could bring back into the mix? Are there any elements or hidden gems that you could re-purpose or recycle?

For example, after doing some consumer interviews about portable wine ideas, I discovered the desire to slowly 'sip' instead of slurp or chug down wine was a powerfully ingrained preference. With this feedback in mind, I revisited all the portable wine packaging ideas from the Ideas Bank and

reintroduced more formats with narrow, sippable openings to my product ideas. This small but significant change ended up making some of the
less appealing product ideas much more desirable.

WORKING OUT WHAT PEOPLE REALLY, REALLY WANT

In your final round of consumer interviews, with your new product ideas
optimised as much as possible, it's time to complete the Consumer Confidence measuring task. Your goal at this stage is to rate the Consumer
Confidence of each product idea based on whether consumers really
want it. After reviewing the likes, dislikes, understanding and improvements of each idea, ask your consumers to position each new product
idea on the Idea Preference Ranking chart, based on how much they
prefer it relative to the other ideas.

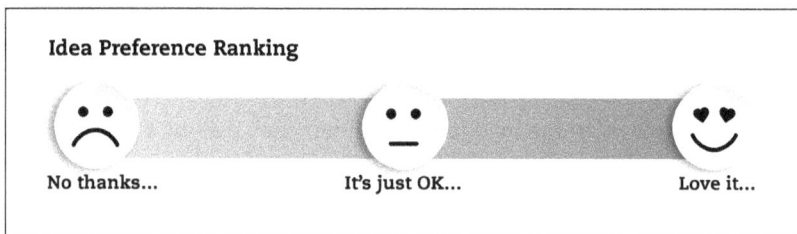

Idea Preference Ranking

No thanks...   It's just OK...   Love it...

This ranking exercise encourages people to rate each product idea relative to the other ideas you show them. It's helpful when you have either
very positive or negatives responses for every idea, as it forces consumers to choose between ideas. Don't let them rank them all identically, so
they sit on top of each other on this chart. Ask them to rank an idea as
either better or worse than another, in terms of their preference. This
tool is also invaluable because it provides a handy visual summary that
demonstrates which product ideas perform better overall.

Here's how to use the Idea Preference Ranking to get to a Consumer Confidence score:

Step 1: Ask each consumer: Where would you place this idea on this scale, in terms of how much you prefer it to the other ideas we've talked about?

Step 2: Ask them to write down each new product idea name on a Post-it note and physically place it on the preference scale. Encourage them to change the placement of previous ideas as more new product ideas are reviewed.

Step 3: At the end of your consumer interviews, it's time to translate these rankings into a Consumer Confidence score. Depending on where people placed a product idea along the Idea Preference Ranking Chart, score each idea based on the following criteria:

- Loved it: Give these ideas a High Consumer Confidence score (seven to ten).

- It's just okay: Give these ideas a Medium Consumer Confidence score (four to six).

- No thanks: Give these ideas a Low Consumer Confidence score (one to three).

Hold onto these Consumer Confidence scores – they're the last vital piece in selecting the new product ideas to progress further with. You'll be using these in the last stage of sense-checking to finalise your ICE scores.

ATTAIN HARD DATA

If you also want to get some hard data measures about your new product ideas early on, then a final step would include a quantitative research approach called Concept Testing. This approach tests how new product ideas perform amongst large groups that are representative of a general population. It gives a statistically representative score for key consumer metrics, such as likeability, uniqueness and purchase intent, which can allow you to evaluate your ideas' performance against comparative industry benchmarks.

Some businesses need quantitative data for their new product concepts to gain management approval to proceed to the next stage of product development, especially if it's an idea that will require a lot of time and investment. If you are interested in, or need, this type of product concept validation, you can't really do it yourself.

Historically, these concept tests were expensive (at a cost of $5,000 to $8,000 per concept tested) and were conducted only by large research agencies. Nowadays, there are lots of cheaper – and equally useful – offers by boutique research agencies, or even online service providers like Survey Monkey, who charge a couple of hundred dollars per concept tested. Just remember to ensure you're getting data on the three key consumer success measures – likeability, uniqueness and purchase intent. Any other data is a bonus, but not essential at this early stage.

Kill or Keep New Product Ideas

Now that we're approaching the end of the sense-checking stage, it's time to pull your ICE scores together and consider which of your new product ideas sit within your Innovation Sweet Spot and should be progressed.

By now, you should have a specific ICE score for each idea, which reflects its Category Impact, Capability Ease and Consumer Confidence rating. How many product ideas have been changed following your consumer interviews? You may need to go back and re-score the Category Impact and Capability Ease ratings for these ideas, depending on how much their product details changed.

I like to capture my final scores in an ICE scorecard like this one:

ICE Scorecard

Product Idea	Impact	Confidence	Ease	Average score
Superfood nut smoothies	5	8	9	7.3
Organic nut loaves	2	8	3	4.3
Natural nut vitamins	8	6	2	5.3
Nut sauces	4	(2)	8	4.6

Once you have done this, brace yourself – it's killing time. This means culling those new product ideas that you've loved and nurtured so far. You're going to drop any new product ideas that don't cut the mustard, so to speak.

Looking at your ICE scores, have you got any ideas with a four or less for Consumer Confidence? In my nut example above, this would include my Nut Sauce idea. These are the product ideas to let go of now. I use Consumer Confidence as my first kill criteria, because it means you're being true to the goal of only creating products that your consumers truly want, not what you can make. This is non-negotiable for any idea progressing into product development. Remember, in the introduction, I raised the importance of determining product-market fit for a new product? If you've tried everything and consumers are simply not interested, you're pushing innovation into the market without satisfying a real want or need. There is no market appetite, and that's the fastest route to innovation failure. So even though it's relatively easy for my business to make nut sauces (High Ease score of 8), because consumer appeal remains low despite my best co-creating attempts (Confidence score of 2), I'm going to drop the idea.

Save your killed-off ideas in a separate file called 'Parked Innovation', along with all your consumer interview notes capturing why they didn't work. Be sure to direct any future innovation teams to reconsider these product ideas and your Ideas Bank the next time your business needs new ideas. Sometimes an idea is simply ahead of its time, and consumer values and preferences do evolve, so these banked product ideas may become more relevant and desirable at a later date.

The Nespresso coffee machine is a classic example of this. In 1986, Nestlé Nespresso S.A. launched a revolutionary system of portioned, encapsulated coffee machines to offices in Switzerland, Japan and Italy. It wasn't until nine years later, when household machines were launched and online sales channels became available, that sales broke even. In 2001, with the launch of a new, striking, ergonomic design and easier-to-use machine, Nespresso generated record sales. And then in 2006, with global expansion and George Clooney as brand ambassador, the business grew significantly by tapping into the expanding in-home coffee culture. Nespresso is now recognised as the trendsetter for portioned coffee worldwide, yet few people realise this seemingly rapid rise to success started over thirty years ago.

For the product ideas you've kept, now it's time to plot them on this 2 x 2 Review Matrix, which shows Capability Ease and Category Impact.

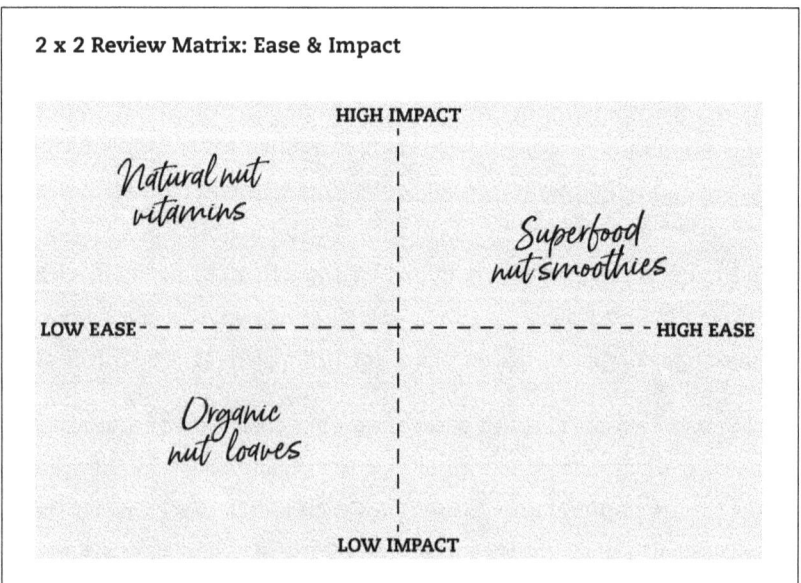

2 x 2 Review Matrix: Ease & Impact

HIGH IMPACT

Natural nut vitamins

Superfood nut smoothies

LOW EASE -------------------- HIGH EASE

Organic nut loaves

LOW IMPACT

Do you have any product ideas that are hard to make (Low Ease score) *and* won't make a huge splash in the category (Low Impact score)? I use this as my second kill criteria at this stage. In my example, this would be the idea for organic nut loaves. I recommend also shifting these product ideas into your Parked Innovation file, as these ideas will be extremely hard to develop and offer little commercial return for your efforts. In the future, when supply or manufacturing capabilities improve and consumer preferences shift, these ideas may be worth revisiting.

I like to keep low Ease and high Impact product ideas in the pool of winning ideas, because as you take these ideas through the product development process, your Capability Ease and Category Impact scores can change with a more in-depth feasibility review and in-market testing. For example, five years ago, the dream of creating personalised food or beverage labels – with a different picture or name on every label – was pure fiction. The idea came up in almost every ideation workshop I ran for personalised products or gifts, because consumers' desire for something unique and specific to them is an enduring want. These ideas usually scored high for Confidence and Impact but low for Ease, and ended up parked in the 'too hard' basket.

However, nowadays, with the technological development in digital printing, these product ideas are highly feasible. Digital printing has variable data capability and can run high quality, smaller print runs without the significant setup costs of traditional offset printing. In 2014, Coke made headlines worldwide by tapping into this technology with its 'Share a Coke' campaign, which had consumers clamouring to find their name among the millions of personalised bottle labels launched. Now, whenever I come across high Impact – low Ease ideas, I keep them firmly in hand and highlight what needs to become possible for these ideas to come to fruition.

Now take a breath and smile.

You've finished sense-checking and have selected your winning product ideas. These are the ideas that are worth progressing into new product development. By this stage, you should be holding at least ten new product ideas that represent a good risk and reward balance of core, adjacent and transformational innovation to fuel future growth.

Key Learnings and Actions

Congratulations – you're on the home straight and ready for the final stage, Stage 5, where you'll learn how to translate these winning product ideas into a long-term innovation plan for your business. But first, here's a summary of the key learnings and actions from Stage 4.

KEY LEARNINGS

- The Innovation Sweet Spot for new product ideas is based on Category Impact, Consumer Confidence and Capability Ease. New ideas are reviewed and scored on these measures using the ICE model.

- A product concept is a simple, fast and cheap prototype which allows you to share new ideas with consumers.

- Qualitative interviewing helps you co-create and optimise new product ideas directly with your consumers.

- Don't expect product ideas to be right the first time. Every product idea will require improvements.

- Allow for two or three rounds of consumer interviews to re-craft and improve your new product ideas before deciding whether to progress them or kill them off based on their ICE scores.

KEY ACTIONS

- Go to: **www.eatdrinkinnovate.com.au/if-bonus** and download the free templates to complete your Stage 4 Sense-Check tasks. These include: What's Hot and What's Not, the Idea Preference

Ranking chart, the ICE Scorecard, and the 2 x 2 Review Matrix for Ease and Impact.

- After your ideation workshop, go dark and keep all your ideas under wraps, to avoid premature idea death by oversharing.

- Use the ICE model to evaluate each of your new product ideas based on Category Impact, Consumer Confidence and Capability Ease.

- Develop product concepts to share with your consumers for feedback.

- Brush up on your interviewing skills and use the What's Hot and What's Not and Idea Preference Ranking tools to capture consumer feedback on your new product ideas.

- Craft and re-work your new product ideas based on consumer feedback.

- Kill off any ideas that score below five on Consumer Confidence or have a combined Low Capability Ease and Low Category Impact score.

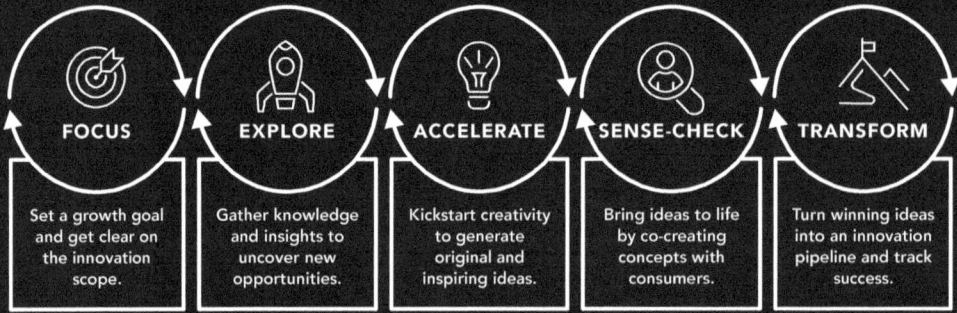

FOCUS

Set a growth goal and get clear on the innovation scope.

EXPLORE

Gather knowledge and insights to uncover new opportunities.

ACCELERATE

Kickstart creativity to generate original and inspiring ideas.

SENSE-CHECK

Bring ideas to life by co-creating concepts with consumers.

TRANSFORM

Turn winning ideas into an innovation pipeline and track success.

you are here

STAGE 5:

Transform

'Change is inevitable, but transformation is by conscious choice.'

– Heather Ash Amara

It's now time to rip off your black ops face-mask and share your innovation feast of desirable, feasible and impactful product ideas with the rest of your business. You've been on a massive journey of innovation. You've gathered insights, found new opportunities, created original product ideas and sense-checked those ideas. However, you need to remember that the rest of your business *hasn't* experienced any of this.

So, we need to catch them up on what they've missed. Otherwise, you'll experience GM-attack. As you may recall from Stage 4, that's when your general manager takes one look at your ideas and says, 'I don't like them, let's change them to…' and all your hard work goes down the drain.

In this final stage of the FEAST framework, I'll show you how to present a compelling case for your new product ideas. This will ensure you gain the support of key decision-makers within your business, allowing you to move into the product development and launch phases.

Gather Your Evidence

If you want to set your product ideas up for success, it pays to be prepared. That's why you need to gather all your evidence as to how and why you have the right product ideas to grow your hungry business. If you're not sure where to start, here are eight steps you should tick off.

These are designed to be undertaken with any stakeholders you need to gain agreement from in order to go ahead into product development. With each step, I've outlined the action you should take and the reason why you should take it.

1. **Action**: Share your innovation growth goal.
    Reason: To show your management team the very tangible innovation growth goal your business needs to achieve – this usually gets people's attention fast.

2. **Action**: Pull up your Innovation Ingredient List.
    Reason: To remind key stakeholders of the agreed innovation scope you worked within – this helps avoid unwanted project scope creep.

3. **Action**: Present your Opportunity Springboards.
    Reason: These demonstrate the fresh insights and inspiring opportunities you uncovered, which ensured you put your consumer at the heart of every idea you developed.

4. **Action**: Outline your top twenty product ideas.
    Reason: To show you went far and wide to generate eighty to one hundred new ideas, leaving no stone unturned, and these are the best of the lot.

5. **Action**: Share the ICE ranking summary of your top twenty new product ideas.
    Reason: This shows you have a top-line understanding of each idea's desirability, feasibility and category impact. It demonstrates a good mix of core, adjacent and transformational new product ideas.

6. **Action**: Show the filmed footage of your consumers co-creating your product concepts with you.
    Reason: This shows you sense-checked your product ideas early, lost the losers and improved the winners, based on what consumers really want.

7. **Action**: Reveal your top ten product ideas and Idea Preference Ranking summary.
    Reason: These show which product ideas are worth pursuing, according to the people who will buy them.

8. **Action**: Ask for approval to build a three-year plan of new product innovation based on these ideas.
    Reason: This will focus your business's time and resources on developing new products to achieve your long-term innovation growth goal. I'll show you how to do this in the upcoming section.

By showing your progress through these FEAST stages, you've taken the ambiguity and subjectivity out of new product innovation. Seeing the progression of your journey, and hearing live consumer feedback, is so powerful – I've seen it sway even the most cynical CEOs and stubborn retail buyers. Why? Because it's hard to argue with your consumers. At the end of the day, they're the ones who ultimately determine the success of your business.

If you've done all of this, the next question you'll probably face is: How quickly can we launch these? Take that impatience as a sign of approval. You're now ready to create a three-year product innovation plan to fuel long-term business growth. In other words, it's time to set the table and lay out your innovation feast.

Create a Product Innovation Plan

You are going to turn your beautiful cluster of winning product ideas into a long-term innovation plan. This will help you prioritise resources and support your overarching business growth plans.

Without careful management, this stage can be like Christmas morning with an over-excited four year old child. In their frenzy to see all their presents as quickly as possible, they tear open the wrapping paper of one gift and move immediately onto the next one – without fully appreciating each gift at a time. This can be a dangerous time, when businesses start churning and burning through their hard-won new product ideas in their excitement to leverage the bounty of innovation they now have. They rush to develop everything in the first year, determined to get the biggest bang for their buck by launching as quickly as possible. This means lots of product development projects are started at the same time. Suddenly there's too much to do and not enough people, time or money. Subjective decisions and personal preferences dictate which projects move ahead. There are also not enough funds to support all the new products, so launch executions become less effective. As a result, the innovation machine stutters, chokes and grinds to a halt.

To make the most of every new product idea you have, it helps to put some rules around what product innovation your business will do, when and why. Never before has the mantra 'fewer, bigger, better' been so important. You goal is to launch fewer new products, which have a bigger market impact and deliver better returns for the business. Setting firm innovation plans will help manage your finite business resources throughout the product development and launch phases. I do this using three highly visual innovation management tools to help plan, communicate and track your next three years of new product innovation. These tools are:

1. An **Innovation Funnel**. This is a three-year pipeline of new product innovation.
2. An **Innovation Plan on a Page**. This is a three-year plan outlining which new products you will launch and when.
3. An **Innovation Project Tracker**. This tracks the progress of each new product development project.

I explain the importance of each tool and how to use them in the following sections.

BUILD AN INNOVATION FUNNEL

An Innovation Funnel is an invaluable tool for building long-term innovation plans. It helps by visualising what new product ideas you have and when you need to allocate time and resources to progress them for launch.

As shown in the Innovation Funnel below, each new product project is represented by a single circle. Each circle is sized to represent its first full year of retail sales, so your business can see how much each project is worth.

Circles are also colour-coded to represent their planned launch year. With these details, an innovation funnel helps you see whether you have enough innovation in your funnel to hit your desired annual innovation growth target. If not, you now have long-term visibility regarding how much more you need to do and which projects you could do earlier or later.

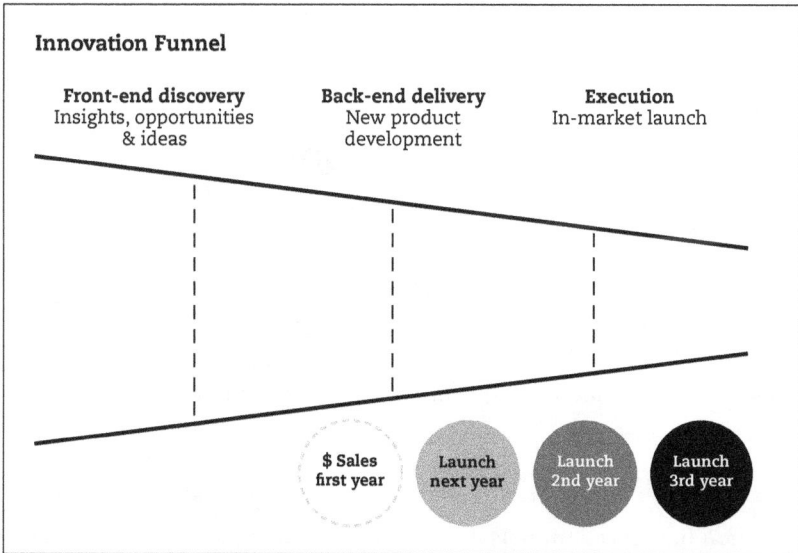

Innovation Funnel

Front-end discovery	Back-end delivery	Execution
Insights, opportunities & ideas	New product development	In-market launch

$ Sales first year   Launch next year   Launch 2nd year   Launch 3rd year

The reason the Innovation Funnel tapers down towards launch execution, and is not a linear tube, is to allow for product attrition. By that, I mean projects falling over, or being cancelled, and never making it to launch.

According to research conducted by innovation coach Phil McKinney, if you want to be among the top ten per cent of successful product innovators, you need to be prepared for a fifty per cent attrition or kill rate at each stage of your product development funnel. This has certainly been true in my experience. Although I may start with around one hundred new product ideas, it can result in just one or two successful product launches. As shown in the following diagram, fifty per cent attrition at each major development stage means one hundred ideas become ten concepts, then five products into development, and just one or two products launched.

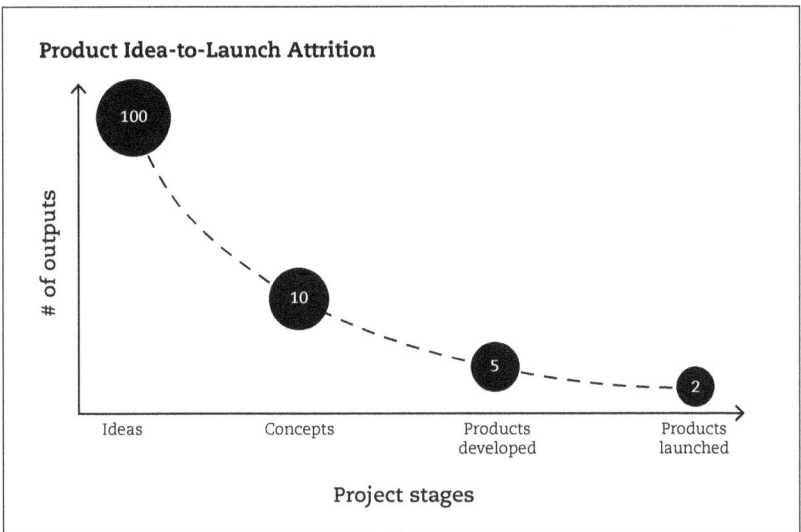

Product Idea-to-Launch Attrition

This is a harsh reality of innovation. Not everything you plan to make ends up being launched.

This attrition rate can be a major challenge for businesses that treat innovation funnels as tunnels. When they develop ten new product ideas, they automatically bank on launching ten new products. This is where in-market success rates suffer, because companies don't expect product attrition during development and refuse to let bad or unfeasible projects fall out of the funnel. And just like you shouldn't go food shopping on an empty stomach, starving businesses end up grabbing anything they can to launch. They desperately push substandard products into the market because, by this late stage, anything is better than nothing. You need to allow for that attrition rate now, so you're not left with an empty pantry and a hungry business that doesn't have enough innovation to feed itself.

The secret is to allow the weaker, less viable, unfeasible projects – which simply don't deliver or can't be made – to fall out of your funnel. In doing so, you'll ensure that you only launch the strongest and best new products. To ensure you're not left empty-handed, though, you need to fill your funnel with enough product ideas to act as insurance against this attrition rate.

To do this, you'll need to follow three steps.

Step 1. Plot the Potential Launch Lead Times

Go back to your top ten winning ideas and review their ratings as a core, adjacent or transformational idea, and the development lead time you assigned each of them in Stage 4, during the Capability Ease review.

Allow for the fact that transformational product ideas usually take longer to develop and launch (three to five years) than adjacent product ideas (two to three years) and core product ideas (one to two years). With this in mind, you should have a rough idea of how long each new product idea would take to make.

Then, divide your Innovation Funnel into three years – next year, the second year and the third year. Create a circle for each new product idea and put it in the year you could make it. You're not locking in launch dates now – you're just getting clear on what you could launch and when, based on the anticipated product development and launch lead times.

Remember that truly transformational product ideas do need a lot of runway time to develop. The other innovation projects will feed your business in the meantime, and ensure you have enough time and resources to get to these bigger bets.

Step 2. Size the Prize

The next step is to predict the size of prize for each new product idea. A lot of people get nervous at this stage, and rightly so, as predicting the sales return of a product you've never done before is tricky. But it's time to do some simple financial modelling to check whether you're going to be in a position to achieve the original innovation growth goal that you set in Stage 1.

You're aiming to estimate each new product's potential first full-year sales return. You may already have your own sales forecasting process, which is unique to your business. Great, go ahead and use that. If not, here are some ways to help you get an early estimate of a product's potential first full-year sales return:

1. If your product is a core or adjacent innovation, I suggest you review the historic sales performance of similar product innovation you've done before, or that a competitor has launched. For these types of closer-in new products, there's usually an existing market benchmark you can use for an early sales estimate.

2. For transformational innovation, this is harder to forecast, as you usually have no other known products to benchmark, since you're the first one playing in that space. In that case, I suggest you make some assumptions about how many retail stores you aim to gain distribution in, and multiply this by a weekly sales rate and desired in-store purchase price. Treat these early estimates as a ballpark guide only – they're not for solid profit and loss forecasts yet – you'll do that once you've finalised the product bundle in the back-end development stage.

However you choose to get to an initial size of prize estimate, don't be overly optimistic. Now is not the time to flash around huge numbers to get the business excited, only to later struggle to deliver. Call it as you see it and be conservative. If the size of prize genuinely looks tiny compared to the size of your current products, now is the time to either re-work the product idea to make it bigger or shelve it.

Now go back to your Innovation Funnel and make the size of each bubble represent the size of prize estimated for each new product idea. You can do this on a whiteboard, hand draw it on paper, or use a computer spreadsheet to plot a chart for you. Whatever you use, make sure it's easy to move around and change things. At this stage, your Innovation Funnel should look something like this:

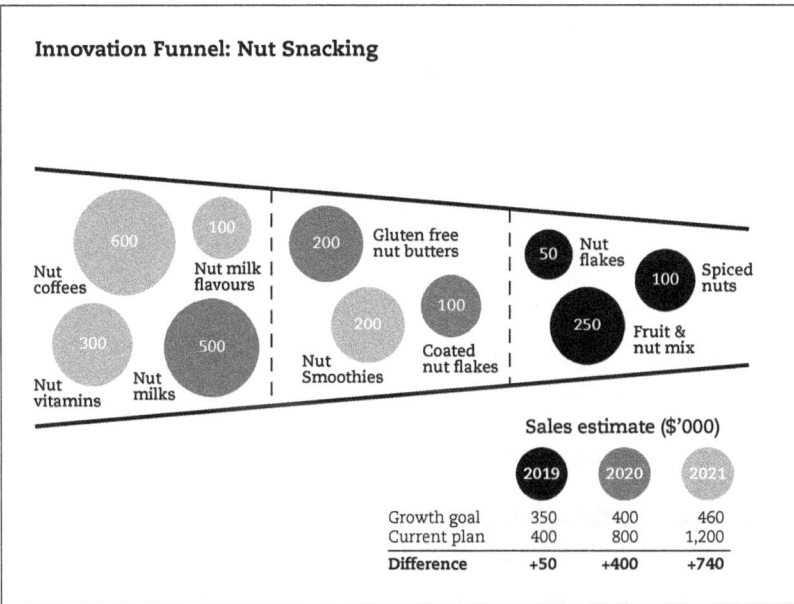

Innovation Funnel: Nut Snacking

	Nut coffees (600)	Nut milk flavours (100)		Gluten free nut butters (200)		Nut flakes (50)	Spiced nuts (100)

Nut vitamins (300), Nut milks (500), Nut Smoothies (200), Coated nut flakes (100), Fruit & nut mix (250)

Sales estimate ($'000)

	2019	2020	2021
Growth goal	350	400	460
Current plan	400	800	1,200
Difference	**+50**	**+400**	**+740**

Step 3. Match Your Products to Your Growth Requirements

Now is the time to compare your three-year innovation growth goal with your size of prize tally for each year. Remember how much you wanted to grow your business with new product innovation? In Stage 1 you worked out how much sales revenue you needed each year for the next three years. Does your Innovation Funnel support this goal? Don't forget you need at least fifty per cent more projected sales in the outer years of your Innovation Funnel, so build in enough extra new product projects to deliver this. This will allow for project attrition, as some new products will prove less feasible or attractive to consumers and will fall out of development.

If you have a predicted sales shortfall in a specific year, try moving projects forwards or backwards in your innovation funnel to achieve your annual sales growth requirements (keeping in mind their development lead times).

Now you have a clear way to demonstrate where the next three-plus years of innovation growth is going to come from in your business. You also know when you need to start working on each project to be able to deliver it on time. No more mad-dash scrambling when your retailer asks for more innovation. No more fighting for internal resources. No more scrabbling around for enough new products when you're planning next year's growth plans. Instead, it's all clearly laid out and in development.

Now that you know what you *could* do, you need to check this against what you can actually execute in-market, as these two things are not always the same. To do this, you'll use the Innovation Plan on a Page.

CREATE AN INNOVATION PLAN ON A PAGE

At this point, it's time to decide *when* you want to launch your new products. Yes, even three years ahead of time. Why? Because you will probably face some very real restrictions regarding when you can launch your new products. You need to factor in these limitations now to help you prioritise which new products to proceed with and when.

The reality is that there's only so much space in the average grocery store. And only so many promotional gondola ends, aisle displays and on-shelf price promotion slots assigned to a particular category and supplier each year. I remember sitting in an innovation review meeting for a large business, reviewing its jam-packed innovation funnel and trying to lock in potential launch dates. The sales director reluctantly pointed out that there was simply too much for his team to sell in the proposed launch period. Yes, you read that right. The wheeler-dealer, target-obsessed sales team, who usually bemoaned the shortage of product innovation, was actually admitting there was a limitation to the shelf slots they could secure, which wouldn't support half of what the business wanted to put into the market that year.

To ensure each new product you create has the best chance of market success, you must refrain from putting it up for launch alongside too many other new products, as it will compete for shelf space, promotional spend, and the time and effort of your sales team. It's far better to give each new product idea enough space and resources to make it as big as it can possibly be.

A way to ensure you do this is by creating an Innovation Plan on a Page. This is a simple and powerful tool that focuses your business on the launch timing of new products for the next three years. It also aligns your innovation resources with your commercial goals. An Innovation Plan on a Page looks like this:

Innovation Plan on a Page

Innovation Type	2019				2020		2021
	Quarter 1	Quarter 2	Quarter 3	Quarter 4	1st Half	2nd Half	Full Year
Transformational							Nut coffee
Adjacent			Cereal nut flakes (Sept)		Nut milks		Nut smoothies
Core	Tropical fruit & Nut mix (Feb)		Spiced nut flavours (Sept)		Gluten-free nut butters	Coated nut flakes	Nut milk flavours

This template shows clearly what you plan to launch and when. It breaks the next three years into segments:

- Next year: Four quarters.
- Second year: Two halves.
- Third year: One year.

This becomes your go-to guide when you communicate your new product launch plans to your business. It differs from your Innovation Funnel, which focuses on your product *development* timings and progress, by showing your in-market *launch* plans.

To build it, you'll need to follow two steps.

Step 1. Confirm Your Launch Windows

Deciding when to launch a new product will be driven by many factors, depending on your business and sales channels, including:

- Seasonality: When produce is available.
- Manufacturing availability and shelf-life: How long it takes to make, and how long you can store your products before shipment.
- Retail ranging dates: When retailers will review new products and put them on the shelf.

If you're aiming for a new product to be sold in supermarkets, you will be limited by their range review dates, which is when they will make room and changes for new products to be placed on-shelf. Although these dates can change, supermarkets are usually fairly consistent about how many new products they introduce in any given year, and which quarter they'll be introduced in for each food and beverage category.

For example, your retail buyer may set one major range review in February, in which it's possible to gain extra shelf space, with a second minor review to replace existing products in September. Accordingly, you have two launch windows per year – February and September.

Step 2. Plot Your Ideal Launch Plan

While consulting your Innovation Funnel, plot out the desired launch dates of each new product idea. Now share this document with your business team for discussion. Can you really execute this much innovation each year? Or do your growth aspirations need a firm reality check?

Remember not to push all your new product ideas directly from the Innovation Funnel to your Innovation Plan on a Page. Keep developing some projects as contingency plans. I've found that, more often than not, I end up using these projects to fill unexpected sales shortfalls from elsewhere, or to plug a gap when a major project falls over. You can also choose to develop these contingency products up to a certain point (before full scale production) and then place them on hold until you need them. This is an ideal position to be in, as it means you can happily build a full pantry of product innovation, with each item ready to roll out as and when the business needs it.

It's important to treat your Innovation Funnel and Innovation Plan on a Page as fluid, evolving plans, rather than with a set-and-forget mentality. They will be subject to monthly changes as your projects develop and change, which is why you need to put in place a tracking process to maintain focus and accountability. This is the third tool you need to make use of.

PUT IN PLACE AN INNOVATION PROJECT TRACKER

One of the greatest principles of innovation is to learn and pivot quickly. Just like a netball player, who always has one foot grounded as they pivot in a new direction with the other foot, your innovation plans are going to require pivoting as you play on.

The easiest way to stay on top of these constant changes is to have regular updates on project status. A Project Status RAG is a tool that indicates when a project is at risk and needs business assistance. It acts like a traffic light (showing red, amber or green) and makes it easy to review all your projects at a top-line glance, and only focus on those projects that are not on track and need help.

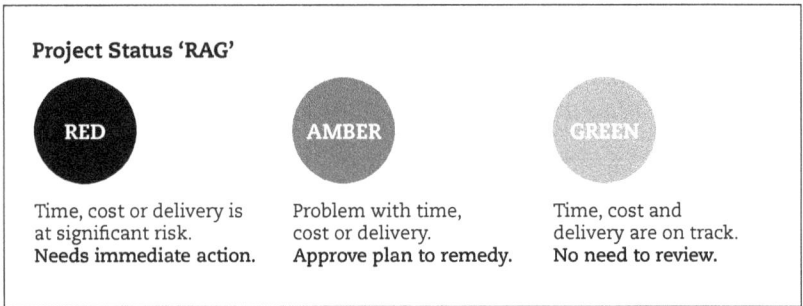

Project Status 'RAG'

RED	AMBER	GREEN
Time, cost or delivery is at significant risk. **Needs immediate action.**	Problem with time, cost or delivery. **Approve plan to remedy.**	Time, cost and delivery are on track. **No need to review.**

Here's how to use this:

Assign each of your new projects a RAG status on a monthly basis. Then, provide your business with an easy overview by collating all your project status details in a simple Innovation Project Tracker, as shown opposite.

This lists each project, what type of innovation it is, its planned launch date, first year sales, RAG status, and a small area for comments to explain its status. Here's an example of what my nut snacking Innovation Project Tracker would look like:

Innovation Project Tracker

Project #	Project name	Type	Launch year	Launch year sales ($'000)	RAG	Comments
1	Tropical nut mix	Core	2019	250	G	
2	Cereal nut flakes	Adj.	2019	50	G	
3	Spiced nut flavours	Core	2019	100	G	
4	Nut milks	Adj.	2020	500	G	
5	Gluten-free nut butters	Core	2020	200	A	Approve new supplier.
6	Coated nut flakes	Core	2020	100	G	
7	Nut coffee	Trans.	2021	600	G	
8	Nut smoothies	Adj.	2021	200	G	
9	Nut milk flavours	Core	2021	100	G	
10	Nut vitamins	Trans.	2021	300	R	Consumer allergen concerns. Propose project kill.

The reason I like to use this particular project tracker is that it can be scanned at a glance to give an indication of how all the innovation projects are tracking and which ones need extra attention. The key thing is to *not* review green on-track projects – let them continue on successfully without interruption. Instead, focus on the red and amber flagged projects. These are the ones that need the assistance, resources and decision-making by senior stakeholders to ensure they get back on-track.

Hold Regular Innovation Review Meetings

If you already run a regular innovation review meeting, try bringing these three new innovation planning tools in to keep the business focused on the longer-term health and sufficiency of your innovation plans. A lot of people tend to get bogged down in the day-to-day details of current projects. These three tools provide visibility of your long-term growth goals, and prompt discussion on whether your innovation plans are sufficient to deliver them.

If you don't have a regular innovation review meeting, start one and meet monthly. Keep it short and sweet – no more than one hour. Don't be tempted to invite every man and his dog – this is a decision-making forum and should, therefore, only be attended by project team leaders and senior management who have the authority to allocate resources and make strategic decisions. Once a month, in advance of this meeting, update your Innovation Funnel, Innovation Plan on a Page and Innovation Project Tracker so that you can use these to direct the focus of the meeting.

A typical meeting flow would be:

- **Project Status RAG (30 minutes):** What needs immediate attention, decisions and resources? Only discuss those projects that are under threat and flagged with a red or amber status.

- **Innovation Funnel (15 minutes):** Has the RAG status changed any development timings? Is your innovation pipeline delivery higher than your growth target to allow for attrition (+50% in outer years)?

- **Innovation Plan on a Page (15 minutes):** Has the RAG status changed what you plan to launch and when? Can you execute these launches in the periods planned?

For example, in an innovation review meeting for my nut projects, I would firstly focus the team on discussing the two red and amber flagged projects to resolve any issues affecting the progress and ultimate success of these projects. In the case of nut vitamins, a major concern arose in consumer research suggesting people were very alarmed about the potential for nut allergens in a healthcare-related product. The product idea of Nut Vitamins couldn't be reworked to overcome this consumer barrier, so it is recommended that the project be killed.

Before any decision can be made however, now is the time for the innovation review group to consult our other two innovation management tools – the Innovation Funnel and Innovation Plan on a Page. It's critical to review these to understand what killing the nut vitamins project would do to our innovation sufficiency. That is, whether we have enough to hit our annual sales goals and fill our launch-plan commitments. The good news is that it's early days on the nut vitamin project, so not a lot of time or resources has been invested so far. The second piece of good news is that our Innovation Funnel shows that although nut vitamins is a sizeable, transformational innovation project (worth $300,000 in launch sales), my business has enough other contingency projects in the funnel to handle this attrition loss, and still be $440,000 over our innovation growth target for 2021, due to the remaining nut coffees, nut smoothies and nut milk flavour projects in development.

A final check of the Innovation Plan on a Page also reassures the team that nut vitamins was one of our contingency projects and hadn't been scheduled for launch yet. Considering these three documents, and the impact on the health and sufficiency of the remaining innovation plans, the innovation review group decides to cancel the nut vitamin project.

As projects are developed and move closer to their launch date, your Innovation Funnel, Innovation Plan on a Page and Project Tracker should remain your key tools to communicate any progress updates to your business and manage any challenges.

Key Learnings and Actions

That brings us to the end of the FEAST framework. Before I offer you my final thoughts and advice, here are the key actions and learnings from Stage 5.

- Gather all your evidence to show business stakeholders that you have the right product ideas to grow your hungry business. There are outputs from eight steps you should collate and share.

- Build an Innovation Funnel by plotting the potential development lead time and full-year sales return of each new product. Then match the timing of your new product projects to deliver your annual innovation growth goal.

- Create an Innovation Plan on a Page by confirming your launch windows and plotting your ideal launch dates, ensuring each new product launch gets sufficient time, support and space to be as successful as it can be.

- Put in place an Innovation Project Tracker, using a Project Status RAG to draw attention to those projects that need additional focus or decision-making.

- Hold monthly innovation review meetings, where you discuss the longer-term health and sufficiency of your innovation funnel, project progress and launch plans by using the three innovation management tools.

CONCLUSION:

Now You're Fit for a Feast

'There is nothing sweeter than what has been obtained at great effort.'

– Swahili proverb

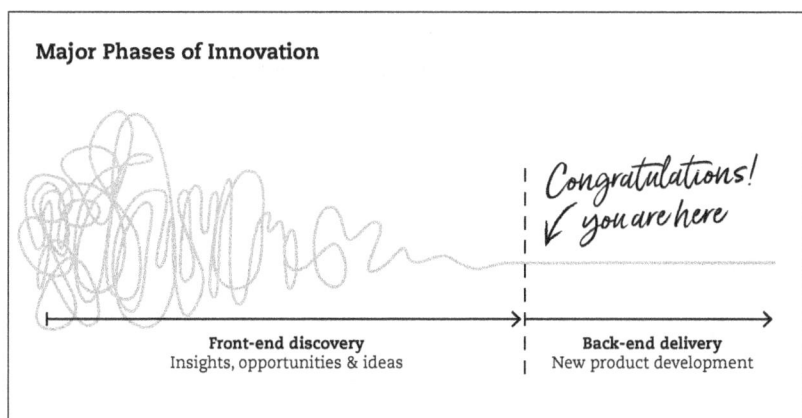

Major Phases of Innovation

*Congratulations!
✓ you are here*

Front-end discovery
Insights, opportunities & ideas

Back-end delivery
New product development

Congratulations! You've made it through the front-end discovery phase of product innovation.

On our five-stage FEAST journey together, you have successfully navigated the exhilarating and exasperating front-end of product innovation. In summary, you have:

- Set a three-year innovation growth goal.
- Determined the scope of your innovation challenge.
- Gathered existing and new data, information and insights.
- Created new opportunities for product ideas.

- Generated heaps of core, adjacent and transformational product ideas.

- Evaluated your product ideas based on Category Impact, Consumer Confidence and Capability Ease to weed out the weak and strengthen the best.

- Turned your winning product ideas into a three-year innovation pipeline of growth to feed your hungry business.

- Set up the tracking tools and processes to regularly review the long-term health and sufficiency of your innovation plans.

In short, you've created a delicious, desirable and feasible feast of new product ideas that should stave off your business's innovation hunger pangs for three years.

By completing these five stages, you have avoided the four biggest innovation traps that lead to an innovation famine in many food and beverage businesses, starving them of successful new products.

1. **Flavour Fatigue:** Flavour fatigue occurs when you continually rely on small, close-in core innovation, like new flavours, which stops providing growth in mature categories with full consumer repertoires.

   You overcame this by: Reviewing your category lifecycle and balancing your innovation types in Stages 1 and 4. You introduced more adjacent and transformational innovation, which had a greater category impact. While it was riskier, it was also much more rewarding for your mature or declining market.

2. **Churn and Burn:** Businesses suffer from churn and burn when they find themselves spending a lot of time and money throwing new product after new product into the market with little success.

   You overcame this by: Not using trial and error to figure out what your consumers want. You followed the sense-checking approach in

Stage 4 to learn early, quickly and cheaply which new product ideas were worth pursuing and which ones weren't, before you invested in any product development.

3. **Empty Pantry:** This occurs when people and resources are focused on the day-to-day business operations, and there are no new product plans beyond the current year.

   You overcame this by: Completing the Warm-up Stage, where you dedicated time and a team of people to work through the five-stage FEAST framework. You identified new opportunity areas and generated original winning ideas in Stages 2 and 3 to build a three-year innovation pipeline, which has set your business up for long-term growth. You used the innovation management tools from Stage 5 to ensure you prioritised the necessary development time and resources to deliver your future growth plans.

4. **Leaky Bucket:** This occurs when businesses are so busy adding new products that they forget to take care of their existing products, which become tired and irrelevant. Sales decline is greater than new product sales growth, causing the business to leak money.

   You overcame this by: Using the innovation types outlined in Stage 1, and changing your innovation balance to increase core innovation so your existing product sales kept humming along. This helped fund your investment into riskier adjacent and transformational innovation that will drive step-change growth for your business.

Remember that this FEAST approach and your new product ideas are not fixed or static. Once you've completed the five stages and start to initiate new product projects, you will need to keep evaluating the Impact, Confidence and Ease metrics to ensure your new products are still desirable, feasible and commercially impactful through the back-end innovation development phase. That is the very nature of innovation; it is always evolving.

The Sweet Taste of Success

Fast forward to three years from now. You've developed winning ideas, used the innovation management and project tracking tools, and successfully made and launched new products in the marketplace. How do you know whether your innovation efforts have been a success?

Most businesses use retrospective measures. These are important for tracking commercial success, like sales revenue, market share or profitability. However, these measures are called retrospective because you have to wait until *after* the event to see if you've been successful or not.

It's like watching the last seconds of a car race when the winner crosses the line. You have no idea what happened along the way, and if your car didn't win, you don't really know why. Did the car have engine troubles? Did the driver go too slowly? Retrospective measures don't identify problems along the way. All you can do is wait for the final outcome and try to do things differently next time.

In many businesses, retrospective innovation measures tend to be things like:

1. Sales achieved compared to launch expectations.

2. Percentage of total sales generated by new products versus current products.

3. Number of product launches a year (for example, three big launches in three years).

4. The return on investment (ROI) of a new product over three years.

For measuring new product innovation success, I suggest you supplement your retrospective measures with some predictive indicators of success. These are like milestones along the way for new product development. If you're watching your racing car go around each lap of the track, there's a greater likelihood you'll identify a problem quickly and fix it as soon as it occurs, so you have a greater chance of winning the race.

These could include measures like:

1. Number of new product ideas generated each year. Are you providing enough fuel to satisfy your business growth needs?

2. Sufficiency of your three-year innovation pipeline (estimated sales return and number of projects in development). Are you keeping your pantry fully stocked?

3. Innovation attrition rates. Are you being realistic about how many new projects fall out of your innovation funnel and how many progress to launch?

4. Percentage of red RAG status projects. Do you have enough people, time and resources to achieve your innovation ambition? How many projects are on track versus off track?

These predictive measures serve as early warning flags. If they're off track, you can redirect resources in your business quickly to get them back in order. Then you won't be reacting to any innovation shortfalls or issues – you'll be proactively adapting and strengthening your plans.

Predictive measurements also ensure innovation projects are visible in your business, so those employees working on them have more immediate measures of their success, rather than having to wait years to see if a new product launch was successful.

What's Next on the Menu?

The beauty of where you are now is that you are set to maximise your new product success. Without FEAST, you were blindly creating new products that you hoped consumers would want, like and buy. Now you know they will. You know what your new products should look like, taste like, be packaged in, and the benefits they must offer. As you move into the back-end of innovation – actual product and packaging development – you have all the right knowledge at your fingertips to start delivering and satisfying those end-user expectations. Be crystal clear on the gold standard you are aiming for as you start developing your packaging, your product specifications and product experience.

I'd developed a product idea for a candy gifting business, which had an amazing response with consumers. It was playful and cheeky with outrageous packaging. A year later, the project team showed me the end product for launch, which looked fun but less wacky than the original idea. The team explained that as manufacturing, supply, product costs, finance, branding and retailer demands all came to bear, the product idea had been changed to be more profitable and easier to produce. Fortunately, they still knew that consumers would buy the revised option, because they had sense-checked it before launch. While it might not have been as outrageously fun and breakthrough as the original idea, the final candy gift box still delighted people and in-market sales were strong.

The real challenge as you go forward is to not lose your way, and to keep checking the appetite of your market. You can do this by regularly touching base with your consumers to ensure your translation of the original awesome product idea to final product experience remains true. Imagine you're behind the wheel of a fast car and your consumer is the satellite navigation. By sense-checking with them constantly, you'll be guided along the right route. Don't ditch them midway through the trip and expect to reach the same destination. Use the consumer sense-check tools from Stage 4 before finalising important product elements, such as packaging formats, product formulation and artwork designs. This will significantly increase the likelihood that your products will be welcomed with open arms by consumers at launch.

I hope this book has provided you with all the necessary inspiration, guidance, tools and techniques to build a deliciously filling and satisfying innovation feast that feeds your hungry business. You should now be set to continue on into the back-end of your innovation journey, secure in the knowledge that you've got some brilliant new product ideas, which are worth investing time, money and effort into as you progress them to launch.

This book is the first step to enable and empower you to achieve successful product innovation for yourself, so that you can whip up an innovation feast for your business, time and time again. However, sometimes it's still helpful to ask a waiter for their recommendation on what to order, so if you'd like some guidance as you make your way through the FEAST framework, you can get in touch with me at **www.eatdrinkinnovate.com.au.**

If you're ready to independently take your learning to the next level, all the templates featured in this book are available on my website – simply go to **www.eatdrinkinnovate.com.au/if-bonus** for the free downloads. There are over twenty innovation templates and tools that you won't need to create yourself and can start using immediately.

I can't wait to hear all about your product innovation challenges and successes, and look forward to seeing your delicious and desirable new products lining the shelves.

Happy FEASTing,

Susie White

Susie White

NOTES

Introduction: Fighting an Innovation Famine

- Barsh, J., Capozzi, M.M., & Davidson, J. (2008). McKinsey Quarterly. http://www.mckinsey.com.
- Castellion, G. (2013). New Product Failure Rates: Influence of Argumentum ad Populum and Self-Interest. *Journal of Product Innovation & Management*, 30, 976-979.
- Cooper, R.G., & Kleinschmidt, E.J. (2010). Success Factors for New-Product Development. *Wiley International Encyclopedia of Marketing*. 5.
- Cooper, R.G., & Kleinschmidt, E.J. (1988). Resource allocation in the new product process. *Industrial Marketing Management*, 17, 3: 249-262.
- Newman, D. (2006). The Process of Design Squiggle. Central Office of Design. http://cargocollective.com.
- 2014 *Food and Beverage Industry Outlook Survey*. KPMG. https://www.kpmg.com.
- Looking to Achieve New Product Success? Listen to Your Consumers. (2015). *Nielsen Global New Product Innovation Survey*.
- Whitbourne, S.K. (2010). In-groups, out-groups, and the psychology of crowds. Does the ingroup-outgroup bias form the basis of extremism? *Psychology Today*. https://www.psychologytoday.com.
- World Economic Forum. (2017). You might be able to 3D print food. But would you eat it? https://www.weforum.org.

Warm-up Stage: Innovate or Fry

- The Story of Grange. Penfolds.com. (2017). https://www.penfolds.com/en-au/about-penfolds/heritage/the-story-of-grange

Stage 1: Focus

- Cole, M.C., & Noakes, M. (2017). The Future of Food. *CSIRO Agriculture and Food Blog*. https://blog.csiro.au/the-future-of-food/.

- Cooper, R.G. (2017). *Winning at New Products. Creating Value Through Innovation*. New York, NY: Basic Books.

- Food and Agriculture Organisation of the United Nations (FAO). 2011. *Global food losses and food waste – Extent, causes and prevention*. Rome.

- Food and Agriculture Organisation of the United Nations (FAO). 2011. SAVE FOOD: Global Initiative on Food Loss and Waste Reduction Infographics. http://www.fao.org/save-food/resources/keyfindings/infographics/fruit/en/.

- Finding Pockets of Growth in the Global Food Market. (2016). *Euromonitor Packed Food Report*. http://blog.euromonitor.com/2016/10/finding-growth-global-food-market.html

- Liquid Breakfasts Up & Going Strong. (2013). *Food & Drink Business.com.au*. http://www.foodanddrinkbusiness.com.au/news/liquid-breakfasts-up-and-going-strong.

- Looking to Achieve New Product Success? Listen to Your Consumers. *Nielsen Global New Product Innovation Survey*. (2015).

- Nagji, B., & Tuff, G. (2012). Managing Your Innovation Portfolio. *Harvard Business Review*. https://hbr.org.

- We Are What We Eat, Healthy Eating Trends Around the World. (2015). *Nielsen Global Insights*. https:/www.nielsen.com.

Stage 2: Explore

- Australian Exports of Cheese & Curd, 1988-2017. *Trading Economics.com*. https://tradingeconomics.com/australia/exports-of-cheese-curd.

- Cheese Cheddar Nutrition Facts and Calories. *Nutrition Data.self.com*. http://nutritiondata.self.com/facts/dairy-and-egg-products/8/2.

- Design Kit Empathy Map. (2017). IDEO.org. (2017). http://www.designkit.org/resources.

- Per Capita Cheese Consumption Correlates with Number of People Who

Died by Becoming Tangled in their Bedsheets. *TylerVigen.com*. http://
www.tylervigen.com/spurious-correlations.

Stage 3: Accelerate

- Carolyn Creswell. Carman's Kitchen.com.au. http://www.
carmanskitchen.com.au/our-story/carolyn-creswell.

- Connolly T., Routhieaux R. L., Schneider, S. K. (1993). On the effectiveness
of groups brainstorming: test of one underlying cognitive mechanism.
Small Group Research. pp. 490–503.

- Eberle, B. (1996). Scamper: Games for Imagination Development. Prufrock
Press Inc.

- Thornburg, P. and Thornburg, D. The Thinker's Toolbox, Dale Seymour
Publications, USA, 1989.

Stage 4: Sense-Check

- Castellion, G. (2013). New Product Failure Rates: Influence of
Argumentum ad Populum and Self-Interest. *Journal of Product Innovation &
Management*, 30, 976-979.

- The Chobani Way. Chobani.com. http://www.chobani.com/ethos.

- Gogol mogul – an innovative product for those trying to eat healthily.
Kian.ru. http://kian.ru/eng/projects/gogol-mogol.

- Goldenberg, J., Levav, A., Mazursky, D., & Solomon, S. (March 2003).
Finding your Innovation Sweet Spot. Harvard Business Review.

- Levitt., T. (1965). Exploit the Product Life Cycle. Harvard Business Review.

- Nagji, B., & Tuff, G. (2012). Managing Your Innovation Portfolio. *Harvard
Business Review*. https://hbr.org.

- Selecting an ICE-Score. (2017). Growthhackers Help Zendesk. https://
growthhackershelp.zendesk.com.

- *Thrive across the full spectrum of innovation* (2015). Happen Innovation
Agency and Consultancy. https://www.happen.com.

Stage 5: Transform

- Cooper, R.G. (2017). *Winning at New Products. Creating Value Through Innovation*. New York, NY: Basic Books.
- McKinney, P. (2016). Managing the Fuzzy Front-end of the Innovation Funnel. S12, E13. Killer Innovations.com.

www.ingramcontent.com/pod-product-compliance
Lightning Source LLC
Chambersburg PA
CBHW020835210326
41598CB00019B/1904